Ride

Cyclist
Ride
The greatest cycling routes in the world

MITCHELL BEAZLEY

Contents

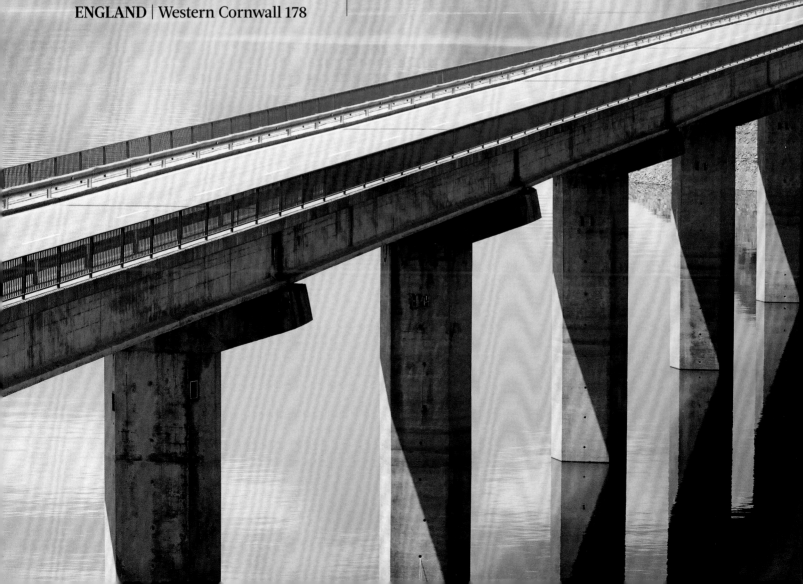

CHAPTER 3:
NORTHERN EUROPE 124

CHAPTER 4:
THE REST OF THE WORLD 182

Introduction

The world wasn't built flat. So it's just as well that bicycles have wheels and humans have legs. Show any cyclist a road that points uphill – or, for that matter, tips downwards – and they will want to explore it.

There are few greater thrills in life than simply jumping on your bike and going for a ride somewhere new, somewhere unexplored. But where to go? That's where we come in. We have picked 50 rides from the pages of *Cyclist* magazine, every one of them ridden from start to finish by our intrepid writers and documented by some of the very best photographers, to help you discover some of the most glorious ride destinations in the world.

There are, of course, the giant European mountain ranges of the Alps, Pyrenees and Dolomites, made famous by the great riders of the past in races such as the Tour de France and Giro d'Italia. But we go beyond those, for example, to what is technically the biggest mountain in the world, in Hawaii; to the mighty Pikes Peak in Colorado; and even to the *lowest* road on Earth, in Israel. And that's in addition to some of the finest places to ride a bike in the British Isles, including the roads that brought Yorkshire global fame when it hosted the Tour de France in 2014.

The choice is yours. All you need is a bicycle.

Southern Europe

ITALY
Dolomites

Renowned as some of the most
beautiful mountains on the planet, the
Italian Dolomites also deliver as tough
a riding terrain as you'll find anywhere.

There can be few better seals of approval
for the region of Alta Badia in the Italian
Dolomites than the fact that a host of pro
riders use it as a training playground. Vincenzo
Nibali – one of only six riders in history to have
won the Tour de France, Giro d'Italia and Vuelta
a España – has often sent the locals into a frenzy
with his appearances here. But even without that
commendation, the savagely beautiful landscape
would be enticing.

The Dolomites are a rugged realm of stark,
serrated mountains, glacial landforms, echoing
valleys and pristine meadows festooned with

Distance: 130km (81 miles)
Elevation: 3,989m (13,087ft)

bluebells and edelweiss. There is a bewildering array of climbs to choose from, but this ride starts in Corvara, nestled in Val Badia at the foot of the horseshoe-shaped Sella Massif. As well as tackling the mighty Passo Giau you will also battle the 2,057-m (6,749-ft) Passo Fedaia, the summit of which is adorned by the sparkling waters of the Lago Fedaia.

First, however, you must cross the Passo Gardena and Passo Sella. Fresh and fun but with a surprising kick, the 2,121-m (6,959-ft) Passo Gardena feels like the glass of Prosecco before the hearty *primo* and *secondo* of the Fedaia and Giau. The climb involves a 9.6-km (6-mile) ascent out of Corvara and crosses

meadows dotted with clusters of pine trees, piles of firewood and mountain chalets. The tarmac is smooth and the gradient averages 6.2% as you climb ever higher into the gnarled peaks.

The descent to the base of the picturesque Passo Sella lasts for 6.2km (4 miles) before the road rises 373m (1,224ft) over 5.45km (3⅓ miles) at an average of 6.8%. The climb hits 9% in the middle, but you're rewarded with sweeping views of the mountain scenery on the drop to the valley town of Canazei.

Next up is the slow, steady eastward assault of the 2,057-m (6,749-ft) Passo Fedaia. The climb averages 4.4% over 14km (8⅔ miles) but you will be hot   >>

>> as you ascend through a natural amphitheatre of snow-covered rockfaces, occasionally diving through pine forests and mountain tunnels. Eventually the azure water of Lago Fedaia appears up ahead like a tropical oasis, the surface shimmering in the intense sunlight.

The Fedaia sits at the northern base of the colossal Marmolada, at 3,343m (10,968ft) the highest peak in the Dolomites. The white tongue of the Marmaloda glacier unfurls down the side of the mountain and a bridge stretches across the lake. At the end is a cluster of restaurants and cafés; this is an ideal spot for lunch.

Sustenance is a good idea before you tackle the fearsome Passo Giau, the approach to which is made even more difficult by a 3-km (2-mile) drag where the gradient hits 18% before an electrifying descent to the ski resort of Malga Ciapela.

There's a sharp rise from the riverside town of Caprile to the mountain commune of Colle Santa Lucia before the Passo Giau itself. This silent, brooding hulk of a mountain is guarded by 29 hairpin bends. The 10-km (6-mile) climb involves 922m (3,025ft) of relentless, thigh-stabbing ascent at an average gradient of 9.1%. There's no respite from the second you start until the divine moment you finally reach the summit. When French rider Laurent Fignon tackled it at the Giro of 1992, he lost 30 minutes and was so crippled by the experience he even had to be pushed on the descent.

The hairpins are all numbered (*tornante 1, tornante 2*, and so on), which feels either inspiring or depressing as your mood fluctuates. About 2km (1¼ miles) from the summit, the stark majesty of the climb begins to wash away the pain. The pass lies in a vast mountain pasture at the foot of the even higher, 2,647-m (8,684-ft) Nuvolau Alto peak, and you're surrounded by sharp columns of rock that jut out of the ground like knives. The beauty of the terrain seems to pull you uphill while gravity does her best to slap you back down. At least the top of the pass offers a panoramic view

The top of the pass offers a panoramic view of the entire mountain region

of the entire mountain region, including many of the distant peaks that you crossed earlier in the day.

The descent is broken up by countless hairpins, so it's worth conserving energy for the final pass of the day – the Passo Falzarego, which rises for 12km (7½ miles) to a height of 2,105m (6,906ft). After the drunken twists and turns of the Giau, the Falzarego seems to slice through the landscape in long, straight surges.

From the Falzarego the climb continues further up, past the mirrored surface of a lake to the 2,168-m (7,113-ft) Passo Valparola, and then there's just a direct run back to Corvara on the SS244. As you head for home it's easy to see why the legendary Everest climber Reinhold Messner once told the *Guardian* newspaper, 'Each mountain in the Dolomites is like a piece of art.'

Distance: 36.5km (22²/₃ miles)
Elevation: 1,678m (5,505ft)

ITALY
Lake Como

Near the glamour and serenity of Italy's Lake Como lies a climb that for 50 years was considered too hard for the pro peloton. That sounds like a challenge...

When you've arrived somewhere unfamiliar at night, you approach the window the following morning expecting the view to bring some clarity to proceedings. Not here, though. Here you will tell yourself you're in one of those annoying dreams where you think you've woken up but, in fact, haven't.

Panoramas like this don't exist in real life. The lake is too blue, the saw-toothed mountains too perfectly capped with snow and the lush scenery too green, bar the terracotta roofs. But after a good hard pinch you will realize you're not dreaming. That really *is* Lake Como and those are the Alps in the distance, with the houses of Bellagio in the foreground.

The ride starts with a tribute to the Giro di Lombardia and its most famous climb, the Ghisallo. Pronounced with a hard 'G', *Gee-zar-lo*, this ascent inspires images of a twisting road soaring up into the clouds. Yet it begins in unprepossessing fashion at the SP41–SS583 junction before passing a 'start' line painted on the road. The gradient isn't too tough at first, but soon the road narrows as it begins to switchback between thick banks of deciduous trees that disguise the gradient, which by now has ramped up considerably. Eventually you reach the small group of houses that makes up Guello, and the gradient eases – for now.

The bald stats for the Ghisallo state that it is 10.6km (6½ miles) long with an average gradient of 5.5%. The key word, however, is 'average'. The gradient early on is a much more punishing 9%, and the final 1.5km (1 mile) also rears up to well over 9%, but in between there is an average-reducing false summit. For 3km (2 miles) you will pick up speed as the road flattens and the lake appears dramatically to your left.

Then there's a sting in the tail until a tightly packed set of hairpins signals that the end really is in sight, and eventually you reach a line on the tarmac saying 'finish'. Here it's worth a stop at the church of the Madonna del Ghisallo, with its four busts outside. The names >>

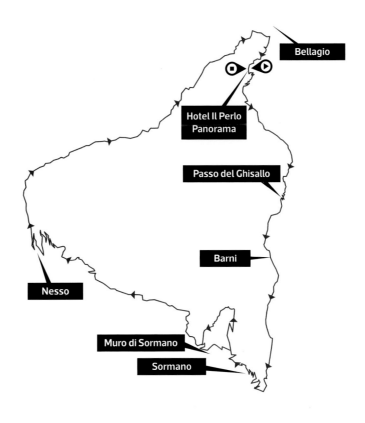

Bellagio

Hotel Il Perlo Panorama

Passo del Ghisallo

Barni

Nesso

Muro di Sormano

Sormano

>> Bartali, Binda and Coppi need no introduction, but the fourth bust is of Father Ermelindo Vigano. It was he who proposed that the apparition of the Madonna (which saved the medieval Count Ghisallo from bandits) become the patron saint of cyclists.

Inside the church is the most incredible Aladdin's cave of cycling history. Signed rainbow, pink and yellow jerseys, photos and bicycles with the names of their legendary riders attached all cover the silent walls. You could spend hours in there.

Back on the bike you'll head towards Asso, a fast descent on a wide road, until you turn right onto the SP44 towards Sormano. Coming just 6km (3¾ miles) after the Ghisallo, the climb of the Colma di Sormano zigs and zags up through 11 hairpins at around 5–6% en route to the halfway point at the town of Sormano itself. From here the Colma di Sormano continues for another 4.5km (2¾ miles), but not for you, because hidden in the trees is your next challenge.

The Muro di Sormano appeared in the Giro di Lombardia for just three years, between 1960 and 1962, before being removed for being too difficult, until finally returning to it in 2012. It might be only 1.7km (just over 1 mile) long but *muro* translates as 'wall' and it's not much of an exaggeration. You need to turn left off the SP44 just after you pass the sign saying 'Sormano' with a big red line through it, and descend for about 100m (328ft) on a narrow side road. The start is next to a large stone trough.

There is no polite preamble to the climb and your heart rate soars upwards as quickly as the road. You're straight out of the saddle and trees crowd claustrophobically around as you negotiate the first corners into woodland, which at least provides some shade from the sun. There are also markers ticking off every metre in vertical ascent that you make. They are horribly close together. The climb has blasts of 25–27%, but it's the Muro's crippling average of 17% that ensures there is simply no rest, no let-up, no chance to relax.

Once you're out of the trees, though, the setting is stunning. Wild flowers fill the overgrown banks, butterflies flap lazily, and there are sprawling views of distant mountains. To a bystander the scene would look so tranquil, yet on the bike your body is inhabiting a world of noise as the sound of pumping blood fills your ears and your tortured muscles silently scream. After that you descend to the bottom, and back to the start of the ride – unless you fancy tackling the Muro again.

FRANCE
Corsica

The starting venue for the 100th edition of the Tour de France
has much more to offer than simply the chance
to follow in the pros' wheel tracks.

It's more than a century since Henri Desgrange, organizer of the inaugural Tour de France of 1903, promised to 'fling across France today those reckless and uncouth sowers of energy who are the great professional riders of the world'. Yet logistics, economics and politics meant the island of Corsica was for 110 years the only one of the 27 regions of France not to play host to the race.

As part of the patriotic celebrations that marked the centenary edition of the Tour in 2013, Corsica was chosen to host the opening three stages of the Grand Départ. It was long overdue, because the island's bewildering range of scenery provides an extraordinary backdrop to roads that could have been built purely for bikes.

This route runs from Calvi on the northwest coast to Corte in the mountainous interior. It takes in the best parts of the jaw-dropping third stage of the 2013 Tour de France (in reverse), including beautiful seascapes, snaking corniche roads and the extraordinary red coastal cliffs of the Calanches. But the route also features some extras that the pros didn't get to enjoy: the 1,477-m (4,846-ft) Col de Vergio (the island's highest climb), the Gorges de Spelunca (Corsica's most dramatic road journey) and the Scala di Santa Regina (a high-speed and challenging descent through a desolate valley).

The diversity of the landscape becomes immediately apparent in Calvi, because in a single glance you can see white beaches, palm trees and, inland, the snowcapped 2,706-m (8,878-ft) peak of Monte Cinto.

The first 40km (25 miles) are gently undulating as you fly up cliffs that never top more than 120m (394ft) in altitude and glide past sandy coves, sea caves and secluded bays, while, below, waves detonate against the rocks with explosions of white foam.

Near the Golfe de Galéria the route darts inland and you cross a bridge over the River Fango. Here begins a stretch that offers a momentary glimpse of the forests of the Vallée du Fango, framed against the stark grey mountains of the interior.

Over the next 10km (6 miles) the asphalt climbs up to the 400-m (1,312-ft) Col de la Palmarella with an average gradient of 4%. It's followed by a gentle 40-km (25-mile) stretch along the corniche road that hugs the western coastline. Here you pass jagged >>

Calvi

Ponte Castirla

Corte

Porto

Piana

Distance: 199km *(124 miles)*
Elevation: 3,400m *(11,155ft)*

The island's bewildering scenery provides an extraordinary backdrop

>> rocks covered in green and orange lichen and dip under the shade of the island's ubiquitous laricio pines. Looking towards the coast you can see rust-red cliffs, pebble beaches, crescent-shaped bays and the volcanic mass of stacked slabs and rocky outcrops that form the Réserve Naturelle de Scandola.

Next up there's a tunnel of gum trees to the coastal town of Porto, which curls around a sandy cove beneath a 16th-century Genoese watchtower. From

here there's a 12-km (7½-mile) climb south towards the coastal town of Piana to take in one of the most arresting natural landscapes in Corsica: the Calanches. These fiery red and orange pinnacles rise up along the coastline like the towering ramparts of a rock-hewn fortress. Some of their peaks have been eroded into bizarre shapes – look out for a heart, a monocled bishop, a devil and a bear – and the rocks change colour in the shifting sunlight, glowing deep red at sunset. The climb is punchy, with gradients of

up to 14%, but the eerie landscape makes every bead of sweat worthwhile.

Zipping downhill, you start a 30-km (18½-mile) inland journey to the 1,478-m (4,849-ft) Col de Vergio, the highest point in Corsica traversable by road. The scenery changes dramatically as you head east and carve through the Gorges de Spelunca, surrounded by steep granite walls, boulder-strewn rivers and rugged valleys lined with conifers and chestnut trees, to the pretty mountain village of Évisa, which appears as a vivid cluster of terracotta roofs amid the greenery.

The expansive views shrink away when you head into the shade of Corsica's giant pines in the Forêt d'Aïtone. There are crystal-clear natural pools here that you can swim in, but it's cooler at this altitude, so jackets and gilets are preferable to swimwear. The stunning Col de Vergio at the top is by no means the final highlight of the ride. The 1,000-m (3,281-ft) descent takes in the stark Forêt de Valdu Niellu, the shimmering Lac de Calacuccia and a rugged gorge known as the Scala di Santa Regina, which meanders for 21km (13 miles) beneath sheer granite walls reaching 300m (984ft) in height. It's said locally that if Corsica is the work of God, the Scala is the work of the Devil.

The route finishes in the town of Corte, where you can stay the night or arrange for a luggage transfer or pick-up. We'd recommend the former so you can continue exploring from here after a good night's rest. Corsica is a place of infinite variety, which deserves to be enjoyed with your eyes wide open.

SPAIN
Tenerife

A favourite training ground of Britain's Tour winners, Tenerife is also perfect for the rest of us mere mortals thanks to year-round sun, empty roads and the occasional volcano to climb.

Located 300km (186 miles) from Africa and 1,300km (808 miles) from Spain, Tenerife is at the same latitude as the Sahara Desert but in the same time zone as the UK. It's also home to the spectacular 3,718-m (12,198-ft) Pico del Teide, a volcano from which a solitary road stretches out like a solidified river of lava.

The Teide National Park, a UNESCO World Heritage Site, is perfect for scientists. NASA tested robotic vehicles on the unusual terrain here before sending them to Mars, and the observatory here is one of the world's best. But the landscape is also a magnet for cyclists thanks to its endless climbs, faultless climate and fitness-boosting altitude. It was on Tenerife's smooth, sun-baked roads that Bradley Wiggins, Chris Froome and Geraint Thomas all sculpted their Tour de France successes. >>

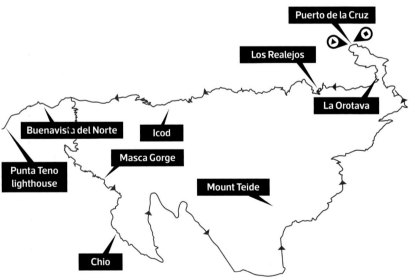

Puerto de la Cruz

Los Realejos

La Orotava

Buenavista del Norte   Icod

Masca Gorge

Punta Teno lighthouse

Mount Teide

Chio

Distance: 188km *(117 miles)*
Elevation: 4,473m *(14,675ft)*

>> This route showcases the geographical diversity of the island, and your journey begins in Puerto de la Cruz on the north coast of the island, the best region from which to explore Tenerife's mountainous heartland. Start early in the day to enjoy the best views by zipping past the beaches of Puerto de la Cruz and loosening your legs with a steady climb to the town of La Orotava at 400m (1,312ft). Then carve through the Orotava Valley with its deep ravines, banana plantations, palm groves, vineyards and clusters of pink, blue and green houses, before descending into the town of Los Realejos. A sharp climb to the town of Icod el Alto at 580m (1,903ft) snakes high above the coastline, offering wonderful views of the Mediterranean as it shimmers in the morning sunshine.

From the cobbled fishing village of Garachico you can take a short diversion to the Punta de Teno lighthouse – the most western point of Tenerife – via a 6-km (4-mile) out-and-back dash along a precipitous coastal road with cliffs of black volcanic rock that plunge into the frothing surf below. It will likely be windy, but it's a worthwhile jaunt to a deserted corner of the island.

From the town of Buenavista del Norte you climb 10km (6 miles) inland through El Palmar, Las Lagunetas and Las Portelas, weaving through lush farmland before ascending into the clouds. Because of its dramatic geography, Tenerife has a range of microclimates. This means it's not unusual to encounter both blazing sunshine and thick fog within a very short distance.

Over the crest of the hill the mist will fade away to reveal the beauty of the Masca Gorge and the smooth, fast descent into the town of Masca below. The only drawback is that you then have to climb out of the gorge, from 600m (1,968ft) to 1,055m (3,461ft). There are cruel segments of 14% that make it a punishing but satisfying climb.

Don't feel too pleased with yourself yet, though, because following a descent into Santiago (where you may want to refuel) you begin the epic 40-km (25-mile) climb up the volcano from 731m (2,398ft) to 2,300m (7,546ft). This is the kind of ascent that has made Tenerife such a popular training destination. It's long – relentlessly long – but the gradient of 4–7% is mild enough to switch speeds, gears or intensities according to your training goals.

On the journey into the Teide National Park you pass vast lava fields, pine forests and rust-red boulders. What with the sharp, coral-like volcanic stones by the side of the asphalt, there can't be a more painful place to veer off the road and crash. The region is almost totally deserted, except for the odd lizard scuttling through the arid scrubland. When the altitude kicks in, it feels like invisible hands are pulling you back downhill. You feel about 10kg (22lb) heavier, and every pedal revolution saps more energy. At this altitude the body learns to produce more red blood cells and distribute oxygen more efficiently – particularly if you sleep at altitude – but nobody said it would be easy.

There is a short, 1-km (^{2}/$_3$-mile) section of cracked, bumpy road. However, it's worth withstanding the posterior pain. Braving this section will enable you to complete a full loop back to Puerto de la Cruz, which simplifies logistics for any visiting cyclist.

Eventually you reach the triangular peak of Teide, the volcano that dominates the island. One side is lined with the wires of a cable car. It's not possible to cycle to the 3,718-m (12,198-ft) summit because the roads only reach the cable car station, at 2,356m (7,730ft), although it is possible to hike to the top. Either way, it has a fearsome appearance, and it's no surprise that the indigenous Guanches people of Tenerife used to believe Teide was the gate to hell, with the devil trapped inside.

The air up here is thin and the climb is hard, but there's good news: all that remains is an epic 30-km (18^2/$_3$-mile), 2,300-m (7,546-ft) descent back to the beach. It is – quite literally – all downhill from here.

SPAIN
Las Alpujarras

With billiard-table smooth roads to rival the best in the world and not a car to be seen, the undiscovered Alpujarras is the hidden riding treasure of the Spanish mainland.

Cyclists love their food, and the roads of the mountainous Alpujarras region of southern Spain appear clean and smooth enough to eat your dinner off. Their quiet remoteness is a big part of their appeal, and this region really does live up to the label 'undiscovered'. Even the Spanish weren't in any hurry to live here, preferring Granada and its fertile plains to the north or the Mediterranean coast and its rich fishing grounds to the south. The mountains in between just seemed like too much hard work.

The villages of Las Alpujarras cling to the Sierra de la Contraviesa mountains that run between the southern slopes of the Sierra Nevada and the Mediterranean. This ride begins and ends in Cádiar, a large village geographically at the heart of Las Alpujarras. There are few stretches of flat road in the region, but cunningly this loop starts *and* finishes with lengthy downhill sections. You can worry about the 3,500m (11,483ft) of climbing in between when you come to it.

Start by heading east on the A-348, gathering speed for 18km (11 miles) before turning right at a roundabout onto the AL-6400. The narrow but smooth road twists and rolls gently between craggy outcrops of rock and scattered clumps of trees before emerging into a wide valley alongside a dried-up riverbed. You pass through two villages before the road starts a gentle, sinuous descent towards the glistening Benínar Reservoir. Beyond that is the first obstacle of the day: the 22-km (14-mile), 1,000-m (3,281-ft) climb to the top of the Sierra Contraviesa.

Turn right over the dam, where the breeze off of the water provides welcome respite from the heat, before ascending a series of tightly packed hairpins. Eventually you turn your back on the reservoir and valley for good, and a short drag brings you to the quiet, narrow streets of Turón. You might like to eat here before continuing upwards into the rolling countryside. The Moors invaded this region, and after they were booted out it took the Spanish king some time to persuade his countrymen to return. Today the area is full of olive and almond groves, pig farms and the odd vineyard, yet the population is still tiny. You'll see far more lizards than you will motorists. >>

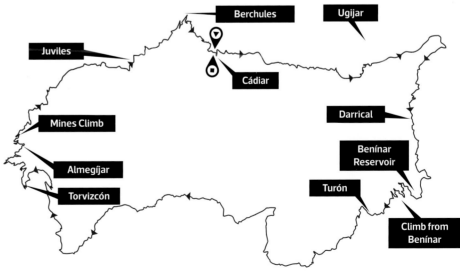

>> Like a discarded ribbon, the road continues upwards, and you will soon catch your first glimpse of the Mediterranean Sea to your left. An hour or so after leaving Turón you arrive on the ridge of the Sierra Contraviesa, the backbone of the Alpujarras region. At this point, you're in for a shock. From gliding over a surface as smooth as an indoor velodrome, you now find yourself bouncing over a road straight out of a cobbled Classic.

After about 5km (3 miles) a left turn brings you back on to the smooth stuff, and a couple of sharp ramps takes you to the highest point of the ridge. Here you're rewarded with endless vistas on either side. To the left are the coastal plains and Mediterranean Sea. To the right are the snowcapped peaks of the Sierra Nevada.

For the next 10km (6 miles) it feels as if you're cycling on the roof of the world, or at least its conservatory extension. It's a pure adrenaline rush all the way to the turn-off for Torvizcón, where the road plunges back down to the Guadalfeo Valley and the A-348. It gets quite technical towards the bottom, the last couple of kilometres (1¼ miles) a series of corkscrewing hairpins that demand full attention.

Leave the village of Torvizcón in the direction of Cádiar and veer off onto the A-4130, which weaves its way down to the valley floor. Cross the River Guadalfeo and, just beyond an overhanging cascade of wild flowers, start the testing 'Mines Climb'. It will ascend 900m (2,953ft) in 13km (8 miles) at an average gradient of 6.3%, with the worst bits – ramps of 11% and 13% – reserved for the final couple of kilometres (1¼ miles). Starting with a dizzying series of zigzags, the road straightens out beyond Almegíjar, then swings left until, just around the next hairpin, the final, fearsome ramps appear like two harmless ripples in the tarmac. Up close, as the road threads its way through the stumps of a former lead-mining camp, they are transformed into mini tsunamis until eventually the gradient slackens off for the final kilometre (²/₃ mile).

From here it's 20km (12½ miles) back to Cádiar and, bar one significant lump to be scaled on the way home, you're in full-on descending mode. You can go all out, or you can enjoy the last of the views.

There's a fortuitous dilemma for cyclists visiting Las Alpujarras. The scenery is so striking, it's hard *not* to enjoy the views. But at the same time, the roads are so enticingly smooth that it would be the easiest thing in the world to shut out your surroundings and concentrate exclusively on the thrill of the ride.

SLOVENIA

Mangart Pass

Do you want mountains or cobbles? How about mountains with cobbles? Slovenia is a stunning cycling location, and all the better for the fact that most riders have yet to discover it.

Distance: 108km *(67 miles)*
Elevation: 3,046m *(9,993ft)*

You'll see them even as your plane starts its final approach into Ljubljana – a set of pale but formidably steep and jagged peaks, like something monstrous from a fairy tale. When you have no clue what the following day's cycling will hold, descending through the clouds to see a sight like this is quite something.

This initial alpine view won't be the last surprise once you've landed and driven an hour west to Kranjska Gora, a winter ski resort near the Italian border that serves as the starting point for this ride. The first climb you'll tackle is the Passo Vršič and it's Slovenia's own Alpe d'Huez, with cyclists from all over the country regarding its ascent as a badge of honour.

The road rises almost imperceptibly at first, until you round a corner to discover it ramps up in earnest to around 11%. And if that doesn't wake you up, the arrival of the first two hairpins will. As the road does an abrupt about-turn, so the surface ploughs itself up into cobbles. Once you are around the corner, the pummelling stops as the road reverts to tarmac until the next hairpin, at which point you feel like you've climbed onto a pneumatic drill again.

After these first two switchbacks, the gradient calms down and the distance slips by through woodland. The gradient is manageable but just occasionally kicks painfully upwards for a few hundred metres, as if you'd planned an interval session. Halfway up the climb, the trees thin and a great wall of pale rock appears to your left. Just underneath one of the peaks is a large hole, and with the sun hurling a shaft of golden light through the mountain it's a mesmerizing sight – until you hit another vision-blurring set of cobbles. The last couple of kilometres of the climb just get steeper and steeper, finishing with a full kilometre (²/₃ mile) at 12%. The reward is the 30-km (19-mile) descent towards Bovec through simply stunning scenery. Thankfully the hairpins are smooth and uncobbled on this side of the pass.

Once you reach the valley floor, you track alongside a tiny river, and such is the awe-inspiring scenery that at times it feels like you're on a road through a set from *Jurassic Park*. You really could imagine a pterodactyl swooping down the valley before soaring up to perch high on one of the crags.

The next climb is more of a road that goes uphill than a real climb, but just before the top you cross a spectacular bridge and turn right onto the second big challenge of the ride. The sign at the bottom >>

>> of the climb is not encouraging: there is a sort of triptych of triangles, warning of bends, falling rock and gradients of 22%. Welcome to the Mangart Pass, the highest road in Slovenia.

It's a dead end topping out at 2,072m (6,798ft), so there is the small consolation of knowing that for every bit of the 11.7km (7¼ miles) you crawl up, you'll also get to swoop down on the return. You begin in the trees, but after just a short distance there's a hairpin that affords a view back down to the huge bridge on the main road and also up to the impressive southern face of Mangart itself.

It's a narrow road with virtually no protection from the drop off the side, and various unlit tunnels boring through the rock bring a blissful cooling shade now the trees have all but gone. There's a sense that as the road winds higher, so it's clinging ever more precariously to the rock, the views getting more and more vertiginous. When you emerge from the darkness of one final tunnel, you feel almost drunk with vertigo as the strip of tarmac teeters on the edge of the world. Suddenly you're up among the prehistoric peaks, surrounded by the summits of the mountains that welcomed you on the flight into Ljubljana.

The road takes a perilous path under one vast rockface to the summit, where you can't help but stare at the view for a few minutes before turning to begin the descent. It's a fast one, too, despite gusts of wind and the darkness of the tunnels.

Once you're back at the big bridge, there's just a short climb to the Italian border. From here the route descends again, into the town of Tarvisio, where you can celebrate conquering the pass with pizza before riding 20km (12½ miles) back to Kranjska Gora on well-surfaced and almost eerily quiet cycle paths. These are not lanes divided from normal traffic, but are actually completely separate tarmac paths running through woods and fields. Slovenia might not seem like the most obvious place for a cycling holiday, but the scenery is easily a match for anything you'll find in more conventional alpine destinations.

Slovenia is a stunning cycling location

PORTUGAL

Douro ey

Portugal's Douro Valley is a haven of quiet roads, vineyards
and stunning views. It would be rude not to sample
the local fortified wine, too.

The Douro Valley is full of wonders, both
man-made and natural. The steeply terraced
vineyards, baronial town squares and riverside
railway, along with the broad, snaking River Douro
itself, make an extraordinary setting for a day out
on a bike ride.

The topography of this region in northern Portugal
– steep hills, narrow valleys and a network of rivers
all squeezed into a relatively small area – makes it
impossible to map a loop that would be manageable
in a day. So this unique ride goes point-to-point from
the river port of Pinhão to the remote terminus of
Pocinho, from where you will return to Pinhão via one
of the most scenic train journeys in Europe, offering
views of the river not possible by road.

The ride starts on Pinhão's cobbles, which give way
to smooth tarmac as you leave town and head up the
hill towards Alijó. The climb for which the gradient
will hover around the 5–6% mark over the next 16km
(10 miles). It's not long before the road wriggles free
from Pinhão's clutter of buildings and you get the first
panorama of the relentlessly undulating landscape and
the crop that has made it famous around the world.

If you don't guess it from the regimented rows
of grapevines extending the length of the terraced
steps cut into the hillsides, the names painted on the
walls confirm that you are at the heart of the world's
port wine industry. Taylor's, Cockburn's, Graham's,
Sandeman – all are evocative of childhood Christmases
when a mysterious and dusty bottle would
make its annual appearance at the dinner table.

Skirting Alijó, the road flattens out briefly
before twisting downwards and heading back
towards the River Douro. Next you cross the
Tua, one of many tributaries that, anywhere
else, would be considered an impressive
waterway in its own right. Here the road hugs
the bank of the Douro for a time before turning
inland and sloping upwards once again.

After a few kilometres of a constant but
manageable gradient, you're forced out of
the saddle by a 12% ramp after the village
of Ribalonga. It only lasts for a few hundred
metres, but just around the corner is another
spike that goes on for even longer at the same
cruel gradient. Eventually the road flattens,
but just as you get used to its smooth, >>

Alijó

Parambos

Pinhão

São João da Pesqueira

Valeira Dam

Pocinho

Touca

Freixo de Numao

Distance: 115km *(71½ miles)*
Elevation: 2,700m *(8,858ft)*

The Douro Valley
is full of wonders,
both man-made
and natural

>> downhill trajectory you turn right into the village of Linhares. Suddenly you're on cobbles that continue as the road kicks uphill and out of the village.

The discomfort is made worthwhile by what awaits you a few kilometres further on: the road plunges down to the Douro in a series of long, sweeping switchbacks that look as though they've been transplanted from the Alps. You won't see much traffic, either. The immaculate terracing of the vineyards is giving way to more rugged farmland,

including olive, almond and eucalyptus groves. It only takes a glance across the river to remind you the hard work isn't over yet, because you can see the road zigzagging up the lower slopes before straightening out into a diagonal line that seems to take for ever to reach the top of the hillside. But for now it's down on the drops for a thrilling ride all the way down to the Valeira Dam.

Once you're across the dam, the climb isn't as bad as it appears from the opposite side, and past those initial hairpins the gradient rarely exceeds 6% for the next 10km (6 miles). You should arrive in the town of São João da Pesqueira just in time for lunch.

The ride out of Pesqueira takes you along a ridge that gives great views on both sides. Below you are neatly ordered vineyards, while above is the more anarchic domain of olive groves. The smooth, sinuous road is traffic-free and rarely dips below 600m (1,968ft) in altitude, before a little-used back road takes you up to a largely barren plateau.

The road heads down a steep, twisting descent, with patches of loose gravel here and there, until you enter the village of Santo Amaro and meet a familiar hazard – cobbles. You'll need to release the brakes in short spurts as you inch your way down what is quite a steep slope. Once you've made it to a small square, the road levels out before climbing for a short distance. Just after the village church the cobbles begin to peter out. This means you can sit down again and just enjoy the final few kilometres of downhill.

The home straight into Pocinho takes you past the towering, metal vats of a modern winery, the smell of the fermenting grapes slapping you across the face like a barmaid's tea towel. There's one more stretch of cobbles and then you arrive at the railway station, hopefully in time to catch the last train back to Pinhão.

Distance: 137km *(85 miles)*
Elevation: 2,475m *(8,120ft)*

CYPRUS
Troodos Mountains

It's better known for its package tours than as a Tour-winners' training ground, but Cyprus is gaining a reputation as a perfect cycling destination.

Cyprus is on the same latitude as Lebanon and a magnet for tourists looking for a cheap escape. Most people aren't coming for the culture (Paphos is the birthplace of Aphrodite, the Greek goddess of love) but for the legendary drinking establishments such as Flintstone's Bar and The George & Dragon. Tap gently up the slope that leads away from the coast, however, and the atmosphere couldn't be further from the sambuca, sunburn and sandals of the Ayia Napa circuit. It's blissfully quiet and the island's interior is a challenging yet rewarding place to ride a bike.

This route is a shallow loop from the coastal town of Paphos to the southern foothills of the Troodos Mountains (the largest mountain range in Cyprus), and back. It's simple on paper, but even the subtle 3% incline on the road out of Paphos is enough to bring beads of sweat to your brow. After what feels like an age, you crest a small ridge and freewheel down into a long, undulating and exposed valley.

In the distance, Mount Olympus (not to be confused with the more famous one in Greece) shimmers on the horizon. The highest point in the Troodos Mountains, it's easy to recognize thanks to the huge white dome – a radar station – sitting on the mountain's peak at 1,952m (6,404ft) above sea level.

Past the town of Agios Georgios the road winds through the rocky valley, and the colours morph from sandy yellow to peach to faded green. Cacti dot the silent scrubland where, in summer, the temperature hovers around 40°C (104°F).

After another 15km (9 miles) the road starts to climb above the River Diarizos before disappearing between two towering rocks near the village of Kidasi. From here the road, which has until this point been following the course of the river, veers off up the flanks of the hills that skirt the valley. You round a wide, sweeping bend and the gradient kicks up to around 10% for a 3-km (2-mile) climb bordered by tumbling, rocky hillsides. The ascent requires a slow, steady rhythm, and your reward is a stop at a roadside café in the village of Agios Nikolaos, where you can eat candied oranges, pears and walnuts preserved   >>

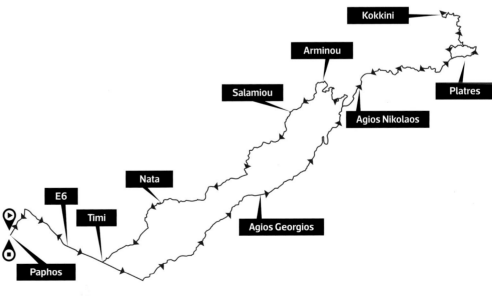

>> in a thick, sticky syrup, in the shade of a patio that provides blessed relief from the heat.

Glycogen levels restored, you leave what until now has been smooth tarmac for a rough, narrow road marked with deep potholes and small craters. Pine and plane trees blend with olive groves and the long-fingered fronds of sweet chestnut. There's a sense that things haven't changed much in centuries around here, yet you're still only 50km (31 miles) from the revelry and Eurobeats of Flintstone's Bar. The road kicks up again, and in the mountain town of Platres the temperature is much cooler than in the valley. Beyond Platres the road ramps up in the vein of a Pyrenean giant – 10%, 12%, 15% – but fortunately the high point is just ahead.

Bypassing the B8 road, which leads towards the ski fields of Mount Olympus, you head west on the E804. The route eventually swings north, and despite its banal name this is the kind of road that would make the motoring journalist Jeremy Clarkson weep with joy. You'll pick up speed as you duck, dive and corner along the smooth, sweeping, sinewy road lined with 500-year-old black pines, along with juniper and almond trees that filter the sunlight. This goes on for 7km (4 miles) to the viewpoint at Kokkini, from where you start the return leg.

The descent back to Agios Nikolaos is fast, and then the road drops down to Filousa and winds its way across the River Arminou. A monster downhill of around 3km (2 miles) is followed by a cruel, rippling road with a series of 20% inclines, and the final 2-km (1¼-mile) Alpe d'Huez-style ramp up to Arminou village is tough. The main F617 passes a host of vineyards, and a welcome 3-km (2-mile) descent takes you to the lowest point on the ride for several hours, the riverbed at Choleria at just 100m (328ft) above sea level. Another punchy climb leads you towards the village of Nata. Here, a clutch of hairpins and a thin, snaking road skirting a reedbed zap every last drop of energy. Then at last you hit the downhill, 20km (12½ miles) out of town, and roll back to Paphos.

There's something special about cycling in Cyprus. There are sharp, stinging climbs that will access the lowest lobes of your lungs, arid valleys lined with claw-like cacti, and twisty, winding mountain racetracks where you can let rip. You could celebrate your ride by heading to Flintstone's for a piña colada, but you might simply prefer a nap instead.

ITALY
Zoncolan

From the first time it was included in the Giro d'Italia, in 2003, the Zoncolan has been hailed as perhaps the most brutal climb in Grand Tour racing.

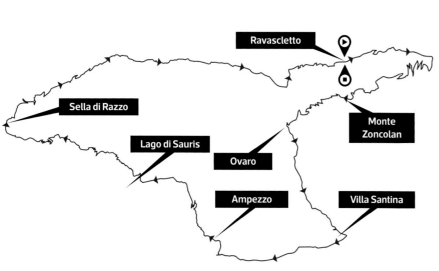

The resort of Ravascletto in northern Italy – where this ride terminates – is beautiful, its wooden-roofed chalets scattered across an emerald-grassed slope. But it doesn't look particularly Italian. This part of the country has a tumultuous history, and the Austrian influence is as clear in the architecture as the Italian influence is in the pizzas, which do look *very* Italian. But something else that will emphatically confirm your precise location is the Zoncolan, which looms beyond the descent from town.

Standing at 1,750m (5,741½ft) high, Monte Zoncolan isn't that terrifying in terms of pure

Distance: 121km *(75 miles)*
Elevation: 3,231m *(10,600ft)*

altitude. It's just the sadistic nature of the roads that lead to its summit. There are three ways up, and our route from Sutrio – which is 8.5km (5 miles) from Ravascletto – averages around 9%.

The lower stretches are rolling, and the trees packed on either side will keep you cool. Then you climb until, after an hour or so, the road flattens out temporarily at a ski station. This brief respite feels oddly tense, because until now the ascending has been the calm before the storm. The final 3.5-km (2¼-mile) stretch is brutal, averaging 13% but ramping up to 23% at points.

The first section, made up of tightly packed hairpins, is truly hard, but the switchbacks at least provide handy short-term targets. The curious thing about the upper reaches of the Zoncolan is that it doesn't really feel like the top of a mountain. You ride through fields that look like they belong lower down, and the trees mean you don't feel exposed in the way you'd expect to be. There's no obvious summit, so you can kid yourself that you're about to arrive at any moment.

You're not. Instead, you round the umpteenth set of switchbacks to find that a long ramp has just revealed itself, rearing up at a hideous angle into the distance. You may find yourself zigzagging up the road, because even though it's narrow you'll fight the gradient in >>

>> any way you can. You'll definitely find your quads burning, but eventually the end of the ramp arrives and you see the summit. Then it's the penultimate turn. And the final turn. And then you'll collapse over the handlebars, sweat pouring, until you recover enough to raise your head and realize there's quite a view.

Ranged out before you are the Carnic Alps, with the beautiful first few switchbacks of your imminent descent in the foreground. Although the steepness on this side never quite reaches the 23% of the Sutrio side, it looks just as daunting. In fact, you drop more than 1,200m (3,937ft) down to the small town of Ovaro, then join the main road (the SR355) heading due south, where you can enjoy pedalling on a relatively flat road at a normal cadence for the 10km (6 miles) to Villa Santina. Here you turn right to Ampezzo and the smaller SP73, which begins climbing through woodland. What starts off as a quite ordinary road soon becomes increasingly precarious, clinging to the scenery with a sharp drop on one side and a steep slope upwards on the other. Then bridges appear. These are small at first, just hopping across a little gully. Then they increase in size until you're crossing a dramatic, gorge-spanning construction with tunnels at either end.

Ah, the tunnels. Long, narrow and dimly lit, with long sections of cobbles thrown in, they wind tortuously through the rock so that frequently you can't see daylight. Upon emerging from one such tunnel, you suddenly find you've been deposited at the head of a stunning lake. It's the sort of colour you'd expect to see in a bottle of handwash claiming to kill 99.9 per cent of bacteria, but backlit and digitally boosted for good measure. As if the colour weren't enough, there's even an abandoned village at the bottom of Lago di Sauris that's occasionally uncovered if the water level is low enough.

There's no obvious summit so you kid yourself that you're about to arrive at any moment

Away from the water's edge, the road begins climbing again and hairpins its way up through meadows towards the two villages of Sauris di Sotto and Sauris di Sopra. This road, the Sella di Razzo, goes on for 26km (16 miles), and although the gradient is a pleasant 4.5%, you'll want something in reserve for the final 3.5km (2 miles), where signs count down the remaining hairpins as the gradient ramps up to nearly 17% for brief stretches. The view here is even more arresting than the one from Zoncolan, and the summit is actually a little higher, too.

Soon you reach a junction, where a right turn signals 26km (16 miles) of exhilarating descent to Ovaro, and the feel of the fresh, pine-scented air rushing over you is liberating after all the climbing. From the junction with the SR355 there remains one last push to Ravascletto.

There is, in truth, a lot more to this ride than 'just' Monte Zoncolan. With its lake, cobbled tunnels and wonderful views, the second half will present you with surprise after surprise.

Distance: 139km *(86 miles)*
Elevation: 3,395m *(11,138ft)*

SPAIN
Andalusia

In a land arid enough to pass itself off as the Wild West frontier lurks this Alpe d'Huez of the desert.

Chances are you've seen this place before. This is the exotically named Tabernas Desert, which at 40°C (104°F) has as little as 20cm (8in) of rain per year. It provided the backdrop for a host of classic 'Man with No Name' movies that put actor Clint Eastwood and director Sergio Leone on the map and gave rise to the term 'Spaghetti Western'. It's not the first place where you'd think of turning up dressed in Lycra, but the region has a unique backdrop for cycling up not one but two monumental climbs.

This route is as stark as the desert: a 140-km (87-mile) loop taking in roughly 3,400m (11,155ft) of ascent divided between the two climbs. It starts in somewhat mundane fashion at Las Malvinas café-bar on the A-349 out of Tabernas. Basically a truck stop, it's handily placed, it opens early and, if you're driving, it's somewhere you can leave your car for free. Head north, then turn left onto the ALP-405, a road you'll likely find deserted.

Looming in a 180-degree sweep in the distance are the saw-toothed mountains that give the Sierra Nevada

its name, but for now you can enjoy a long, easy run-in to get yourself warmed up. At this relatively low altitude of 400m (1,312ft), olive and almond trees line the edges of the road, with only the odd ramshackle house set back among the groves.

Nearing the base of the first ascent – a small village called Velefique – the flora changes noticeably, and with it the climate. Prickly pear plants jut out between clumps of spiky grass, and the air takes on a chillier crispness. The Alto de Velefique climb gains 1,040m (3,412ft) of elevation over 13km (8 miles), with gradients dipping in and out of double figures, making it very similar to Alpe d'Huez (see page 86). It will *feel* very similar, too, as your legs start to twinge.

Graffiti adorns the tarmac, a throwback to the climb's appearances in the Vuelta a España. But that's a minor distraction once you reach the meat of the climb. There, steep rises and the occasional all-too-brief flatter section connect hairpin after hairpin. Once you finally reach the top, the views are   >>

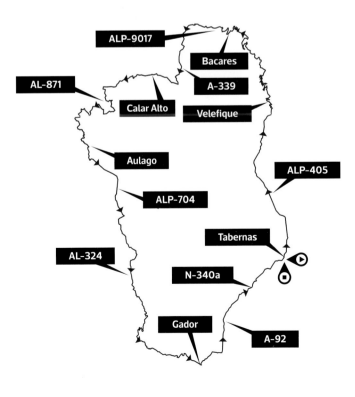

ALP-9017
Bacares
AL-871
A-339
Calar Alto
Velefique
Aulago
ALP-405
ALP-704
Tabernas
AL-324
N-340a
Gador
A-92

>> expansive. Below your 1,860-m (6,102-ft) elevation lies a scorched green basin encircled by a haze of tawny mountains. It looks like God has drained the sea and turned a massive lamp on the coral.

The descent to the tiny village of Bacares is one of those gloriously long roads that you could ride down for hours without getting bored (although you might get cold, so a gilet, arm-warmers and even gloves are a good idea). Watch out for some intriguing holes in the scenery, because dotted around these hillsides and beyond are hundreds of caves – remnants from the Moors' invasion in the eighth century. You can still buy caves in Spain, and they're not too expensive.

Bacares is a good spot to take some sustenance, and then it's on to the second climb, up to Calar Alto. The highest peak in the Sierra de Los Filabres Mountains, it's another savage beast that, like the Alto de Velefique, enjoys both Vuelta a España and first-category status. This climb is much straighter than the first one, and it offers little respite save for a tantalizing plateau just past halfway. Don't go too hard, because the first section averages 10% and will leave you overheating long before the road flattens and even descends for a stretch.

Further up the climb, the fir trees relinquish their hold on the soil. This leaves you riding through a moonscape until, appropriately, the sparkling domes of the Calar Alto Observatory hove into view as you near the summit. At 2,168m (7,113ft) this marks the highest point of the route.

From the crest beside the observatories, it's a sizeable downhill run followed by a long drag back to the start at Las Malvinas café-bar. After toiling at such an arduous pace, it's a blessed relief to get up some decent speed. And at an average of 5% over 30km (18½ miles), the descent towards Aulago is a rare road of smooth tarmac, hemmed in by rushing stone cliffs on one side and sheer drops on the other. On this side of the Sierra de Los Filabres, the yellow hues seem brighter and the greys more muted, so the route is harder to discern. It helps to have a bike computer to map out the road, allowing you to predict each corner and throw the bike in appropriately. Just beware of the goats that abound like little bearded mountain hooligans.

In any other country, on any other road, you'd be more likely to see a car coming in the opposite direction, but here you will probably be able to count the number of vehicles you've seen on one hand, and still have a finger left to flip those goats the bird. This is one deserted desert, but the riding is abundant.

SPAIN

Covadonga

In the Picos de Europa Mountains lurks a climb of legend, which the Vuelta a España has visited 19 times. Find out for yourself what the professionals have to endure on the Covadonga.

This unspoiled part of northern Spain is notorious for fickle weather thanks to its proximity to the coast and cloud-baiting mountains rising to 2,650m (8,694ft). Even in midsummer, wise visitors arrive with a healthy we'll-take-what-we-get attitude. But don't let that put you off, because this really is an undiscovered cycling paradise.

It's also home to the Covadonga, a climb that rises 1,135m (3,724ft) with prolonged sections at 15%, which has entered legend as one of the toughest and most beautiful in the Vuelta a España. This route isn't a loop because the Lagos de Covadonga (the full name of the climb, taken from the two Lakes of Covadonga) is an up-and-back road, which means that once you've reached the summit you get to enjoy it in reverse.

Cangas de Onís is an ideal base at the foot of the climb, but this route starts after a trip by car to Potes. Leave your car here and then take a right turn onto the N-621, which signals the start of the ascent to the San Glorio Pass, just south of the Picos de Europa National Park. The gradient hovers at a warm-up-friendly 2%, and it's a majestic scene as you rise further into the Picos de Europa mountain range, even as the incline creeps up to around 6% and lingers there until the summit.

This part of the Iberian peninsula is called España Verde, meaning 'Green Spain'. The upside of the variable climate is that nature runs well-watered riot, with trees, grass, moss and lichen in full flush right to the top of the mountains, and green seeming to ooze out of every rock. It's a long way from the scorched earth found further south. Oak, beech and lime forests extend into the distance, with meadows nurturing a wealth of wildlife. Yellow broom flowers spread over the hillsides, and purple thyme adds its own flashes of colour and whiff of scent to the landscape.

The road surface is impeccably smooth, and cars are as rare as clouds, heralding a serene entry into the mountains, as you steadily dispatch the San Glorio. Then there's a 28-km (17-mile) descent across the plateau towards Riaño. The road surface has taken on a pale complexion stained with red – it has to do with iron seeping from the rocks – and its cracks testify to the harsh winter conditions.

The plateau levels out at 1,100m (3,609ft) and soon you arrive at the spectacular　　　>>

Lagos de Covadonga

Cangas de Onís

Los Beyos gorge

Potes

San Glorio

Riaño

Distance: 157km *(98 miles)*
Elevation: 2,932m *(9,619ft)*

>> Riaño Reservoir. This was created in the 1980s with the construction of a dam that submerged the original village of Riaño, which was rebuilt in its current position next to the lake. Then it's on to a 5-km (3-mile) rise before the next descent, which lasts for 50km (31 miles) and reduces your altitude by 1,200m (3,937ft). It's fast at first, and then at a steadily decreasing gradient all the way to Cangas de Onís in the shadow of the Covadonga. You'll find that the road surface has deteriorated even more, and clusters of potholes 20cm (8in) deep indicate that the warning signs about falling rocks are not just for decoration. But the pace is fast and the corners sweeping as you barrel along in high-speed payback for the long San Glorio ascent that started the day.

You are now in the Los Beyos Gorge, and there are plenty of villages to choose between for a lunch stop before tackling the Covadonga. This, incidentally, is where the great Miguel Induráin's career effectively came to an end when he abandoned the 1996 Vuelta at the foot of the climb. Although the road out of Cangas de Onís is the official start of the climb, the first 4km (2½ miles) average only 1.5%. Don't be fooled.

The turning point is the cave with the Basilica of the Virgin Mary, which gave the two lakes, the Lagos de Covadonga, their name (taken from the Latin Cova Dominica, meaning 'Cavern of the Lady'). From here the road kicks up to 8% for an arduous kilometre (⅔ mile), then 10.8% for the next, then 10.6%. It's an engaging climb, though, as the steep early stages skirt and traverse the contours of the lower slopes, with varied corners that only gradually evolve into the familiar pattern of alternating straights and hairpins.

Covadonga has a reputation for its cruel ramps, however, and after a couple of 'rest' kilometres, averaging 8.6% and 8.3%, the incline increases to 10%, then 12.5% for a kilometre (⅔ mile) and then 15% for 800m (½ mile). By this point you're likely to be enshrouded in mist, but it's also possible that by the time you finally reach the summit – after a 500m-

(1/3 mile-) downhill section followed by a final 12% kilometre (2/3 mile) – the mist will dissipate to reveal the Picos de Europa Mountains in all their green and rocky glory, punctuated by the two lakes that give the climb its name. The last thing you want after all that climbing is to have your breath taken away, but you don't really have a choice. And you have plenty of time to catch it again on the way back to Cangas de Onís and on to the finish at Potes.

This really is an undiscovered cycling paradise

Distance: 148km *(92 miles)*
Elevation: 3,248m *(10,656ft)*

ITALY
Sicily

With steep climbs, cobbled descents and the constant threat of a volcanic eruption, this Sicilian adventure is a true epic.

One sight dominates the Sicilian horizon: Mount Etna. Chances are you've never ridden up an active volcano before, and it's certainly not everywhere that the earth beneath you might begin to shake at any moment. But while Etna, with a height of 3,350m (10,991ft), will be in sight for practically this entire route, there hasn't been a 'major' eruption since 1992, and there's a lot more to this island than lava.

The ride starts from Zafferana Etnea, and immediately pitches you onto a 17-km (10½-ft) climb up the Strada Provinciale 92, in the tourist area known as Etna Sud. There are only two ways to reach the summit by road: the one you're on now, in the south, and one on its north side. The plan is to take on both ascents at each end of the ride. This southern ramp is relentless, with an average gradient of around 7.5%, and you'll be feeling the burn in your legs long before the road peaks at around 2,000m (6,562ft).

You'll have company, too. Etna is a popular tourist destination, so there will be plenty of buses snaking their way up the climb ahead of you, the sun catching their reflective windows like tiny flashlights spelling out Morse code for 'you've got a long way to go'.

Having completed the last of the road's long, traversing zigzags, you finally crest the top. There's an instantly noticeable breeze, so you may want to pull over to slip a gilet on and take a good look at the smoking crater for the first time.

From here the descent snakes off down the barren, mostly jet-black lava flows that dominate the landscape, and this first downhill of the day delivers a welcome shot of adrenaline. The road is in great condition because, in these parts, resurfacing is a fact of life. On one hairpin you pass a house almost buried in solidified lava, with only its roof visible above the jagged landscape. Home insurance can't be cheap.

All too soon you're at the bottom, where you turn right onto minor roads. The next climb is narrow as you continue arcing around Etna, and the gradient varies dramatically, mostly rolling but with occasional steep ramps. Then suddenly you're descending again, through tunnels formed by the abundance of chestnut trees. Watch out for the spiky carcasses to avoid punctures. >>

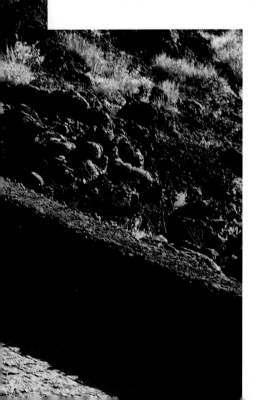

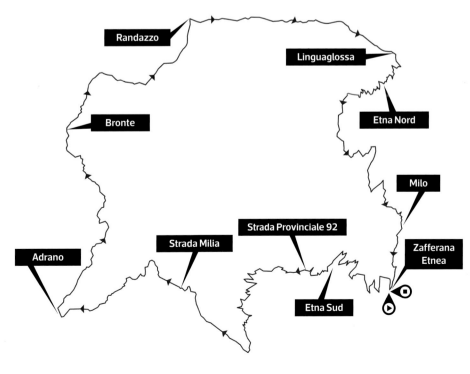

>> **Next you pass through the outskirts of Adrano,** the first major town of the route so far, before a short spell on the main arterial road, Strada Statale 284, around Etna's western side. Just before the village of Sacro Cuore you turn to face the mountain and begin the climb to the Etna National Park.

A short distance past the gates, the tarmac runs out and turns to gravel. The tracks up here are passable on road bikes, but only with a fair degree of care, and the higher you climb the more they become a softer, ash-like texture. It will start to feel as though you're riding on sand.

Soon another gate leads you to the descent, which is something quite special. Cobbles – or rather large slabs of black volcanic rock – are laid out in two parallel strips like the flaming tyre tracks left behind by the DeLorean in the film *Back to the Future*. It's jarring, and you'll be tempted to keep your eyelids half shut for fear of your eyeballs falling out of their sockets, but it's also exhilarating. Just remember to look up occasionally and take in the views of the blackened moonscape before you.

Eventually you arrive in the town of Bronte, which is an ideal place to stop for lunch. Once you've refuelled, there's another short stretch on the 284 towards Randazzo, but you peel right just before the town to follow Etna's curve on minor roads again.

One final ascent awaits you, and it's a rolling, tiring road to the base of Etna Nord. Over your right shoulder the mighty volcano looms, and far off to the left is the mountain range that fills Sicily's northernmost tip, gradually falling into shadow.

You turn just before Linguaglossa to start the climb. The early slopes are wooded, hiding from view the vastness of Etna's northwestern side, but very soon the landscape opens out. Passing shuttered roadside cafés and houses makes the climb feels ominously deserted in the now chilly evening air.

The tourists will have long gone when you summit Etna for the second time, leaving you alone to admire views of the distant mountains turning pink in the setting sun. All that stands between you and a hot shower now in Zafferana Etnea is the descent on the Via Mareneve, which translates as 'the road to the sea'. Rest assured that when you get there, Etna will still be with you, looming large in the dusk. In Sicily, Etna is *always* with you.

GREECE
Crete

With guaranteed sun, winding hairpin roads and just the local goats for company, Crete is a cycling destination worthy of Zeus himself.

Distance: 125km *(78 miles)*
Elevation: 2,735m *(8,973ft)*

It's high up the list for holidaymakers seeking cheap food, baking sun and glassy waters, but Crete barely registers as a destination for road cyclists. This is odd, because it really does have all the ingredients needed, so long as you choose the right time of year to go. In midsummer, temperatures soar to well over 40°C (104°F), with barely enough rain to sustain a cactus. But if you visit in the low season – spring or autumn – you'll find conditions that are near perfect. There are very few tourists and they mainly keep themselves and their hire cars to the northern coasts, leaving the interior of the largest Greek island and its relatively undeveloped southern side almost deserted.

This ride starts to the south of Chania, Crete's second-largest city and its former capital, in the northwest of the island, where the road from Roustika forks right towards Velonado. If you get here by car or van, you'll be able to drive back to the city later on, having completed a 125-km (78-mile) loop that takes in some beautiful coastline, the jaw-dropping interior and an out-and-back ascent that's worth the admission price on its own.

The roads have an empty, almost abandoned feel as they slice through a beautiful yet sparse landscape. Crete is hilly but not especially mountainous. Yet in springtime, orange blossom and vibrant carpets of wild flowers are set against snowcapped peaks. It has the feel of an Alpine retreat and the scent of a spa weekend.

The climb towards the village of Kallikratis is a gentle 5% lasting around 9km (6 miles), and early in the day it's a tranquil affair. Out towards the horizon a few birds of prey hang above the valley floor, and as you crest the top a perfect set of tight hairpins shimmers into view, cascading down the other side of the climb towards the Libyan Sea. It's hard to fathom why cyclists aren't coming here in their droves as you pass through the Perisinaki National Park and turn right to follow the road down to Kapsodasos.

At the T-junction at the bottom of the hairpins, go right and follow the road to Hora Sfakion, signposted 'Chora Sfakion – 4'. What follows is the jewel in this part of the island's crown: a 14-km (9-mile) stretch of road that snakes from the town of Hora Sfakion up to the Aradaina Bridge, a landmark in these parts as a feat of engineering that spans the island's deepest gorge. Rising from close to sea level to over 600m (1,968ft), this stretch is an aggressive beast, and >>

>> within minutes you're grinding up an 8% incline, with tumbling cliffs to your left and great charcoal-grey swathes of road rearing up to your right. Past Anopolis you can enjoy a race – and the spectacular view – across the bridge, before turning around for a joyous descent back to Hora Sfakion. This one stretch has everything a cyclist could wish for. It's long, steep and wide, with great views, and is wholly unbothered by traffic – a genuine playground.

Back at sea level, you can take time for lunch before heading home on a road that now seems twice as long and twice as slow. But then there's one more surprise in store in the form of a sharply rising climb that wends through the base of Kotsifou Gorge and back to the island's interior, and the finish. To be precise, you retrace your steps to Kapsodasos and take a right, signposted Fata Morgana. Head downhill to take in the castle at Frangokastello on the coast, then rejoin the main road towards Skaloti. From there, follow the main road to Sellia, north up the gorge. At the junction, bear left (signposted Kali Sikia) and follow that road back to the start.

Millennia of gushing water incised a thin slit in the mountainside, leaving behind a gorge as stunning as anything you've seen all day. The road is elevated slightly above the waterline with a chapel carved into the foot of the gorge's towering entrance. From the outside, it's a rustic yet ornate affair, quarried from the ruddy red and yellow local stone, with its main vestibule etched deep into the rock. Inside, the scent of incense mingles with damp-smelling air, wafting around the paintings of saints and other relics that adorn the walls. There's an air of history and secrecy to the chapel, along with its rudimentary charm and indisputable beauty. In fact, the more you look at it, the more you can't help thinking just how well this ancient place sums up the island it's on: a picturesque if obvious facade from without, and a trove of unseen riches from within.

You don't really need your swimsuit. Crete has an abundance of hidden treasures and all you need to discover them is your bike and a sense of wonder.

The roads have an empty, almost abandoned feel

ITALY

Sardinia

While not as well known for its cycling as some of its
Mediterranean neighbours, Sardinia offers rich
pickings for the intrepid rider.

Maps are beautiful things. Their contours,
lines and symbols chart history, along with
topography, and record detail as well as
distance. Even the local tourist office's free hand-out,
such as the one you can pick up in Sardinia, is packed
with more intrigue and romance than the flashiest
GPS device could ever hope to encompass.

There's just one problem. Sardinia offers a vast
array of amazing roads and stunning views. Medieval
castles, seaside marinas, spectacular coastal corniches
and various centuries-old historical monuments,
including Spanish watchtowers and megalithic tombs,
all compete for your attention. It's hard to draw up a
route short enough to squeeze into one day.

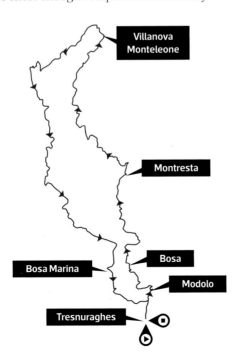

The solution to that is to stay for a week, or more,
but this route will act like a roster of 'greatest hits' to
introduce you to this wondrous isle. Sardinia might
not have the roadie reputation or heritage of other
Mediterranean islands such as Mallorca and Corsica.
However, it has roads and landscapes that are just as
impressive, as you're about to find out.

This circular route starts in Tresnuraghes, and as
you leave the village you're presented with a panorama
of Sardinia's west coast and its rippling, scorched
hills. Follow the road down to the River Temo and the
beautiful, bustling town of Bosa. After crossing a stone
bridge you enter a maze of narrow, cobbled streets
and tall, pastel-coloured buildings. There's a 12-km
(7½-mile) climb coming up, so try to ignore the locals
enjoying coffee, alfresco dining or wine.

The start of the climb takes you tantalizingly close to
the grey, bleak castle that dominates the hillside above
Bosa. Beneath its 800-year-old walls, a row of trestle
tables is dispensing wine, food and happiness to the
tourists, but the scene is callously snatched away from
you as the road veers sharply to the left.

As you climb you'll see the hills and ridges of the
island extending eastwards. The usual signs of
civilization – pylons, radio masts, chimneys, the
smudge of a village or distant blur of a motorway – are
all missing. It's just a rolling patchwork of scrubland,
forests and barren slopes. The emptiness is shocking.

The ascent is not especially steep, but the lack of
traffic, road furniture or buildings means it seems to
drag on for ever. You soon lose sight of the Sardinian
Sea behind you. Ahead of you, a section of false flat
punctuates the route before thrusting upwards   >>

Distance: 102km *(63 miles)*
Elevation: 2,111m *(6,926ft)*

The road unspools
down to the sea
in a labyrinthine
series of curves
and hairpins

>> once more. Eventually, however, you arrive at the village of Montresta, perched on a slope overlooking forests of cork and oak trees. Here also grows a plant, asphodel, the bitter scent of which has been acting like a Vicks inhaler all the way up the climb.

The road plunges downhill for a few kilometres before a sharp left turn and the resumption of duties in the small ring as you commence an even longer, 15-km (9-mile) ascent that will take you up to a

ridge and the highest point of our route. The spine of the ridge, which offers sweeping views of Sardinia's interior, which is dominated by flat-topped mountains rising from lush valleys. The only sign of civilization is a church, standing on its own in the middle of nowhere.

Cresting the next rise, you're reunited with the view of the sea. A bit further on is the modern hilltop town of Villanova Monteleone. The road continues to the popular seaside resort of Alghero, but you'll turn

off and ease out of the saddle for another short but testing climb. At the top there's a spectacular view of the coast, but it's not the turquoise seas or distant mountains across the Bay of Alghero that will catch your attention. Directly below is something far more exciting: the road unspooling down to the sea in a long and labyrinthine series of curves and hairpins. On the map, it doesn't merit a number. It doesn't even connect two settlements. It joins one bit of emptiness to another. There are some roads for which even maps can't capture their exhilarating, magical nature.

Needless to say, the descent is a delight, and near the bottom you join the coast road back to Bosa. The fun hasn't finished yet, though, because this 36-km (22-mile) stretch is a rollercoaster, cresting rugged cliffs and skirting remote coves. The ridge above is dotted with the ruins of watchtowers built by the Spanish during their 400-year rule over the island.

Instead of retracing your route through the picturesque streets of Bosa, you'll now continue for a couple of kilometres along the coast, where the road comes to an abrupt end at a huge wall of rock. The final 7km (4 miles) of our ride back to Tresnuraghes will be solidly uphill, 10% in parts, with contour lines squeezed together on the map that can in no way do justice to the majesty of Sardinia's terrain.

SPAIN
Mallorca

The island of Mallorca is a playground for cyclists, and the main attraction for them has to be the twisting ribbon of road that is Sa Calobra.

Sa Calobra

Lluc

Puig Major

Sóller

Caimari

Selva

Deià

Valldemossa

Alaró

Llosetta

S'Esgleieta

There are climbs with amazing views, roads with rustic charm and mountains so severe we never forget them. But there is no road as stunning as Sa Calobra.

Actually, Sa Calobra isn't a road at all, but a port village on the northern coast of Mallorca. Out of the village, the road up to Coll dels Reis winds over and through the rock formations of the Tramuntana range like brushstrokes on a canvas, and over time this road has come to be known by cyclists simply as Sa Calobra.

The only way to get to the bottom of the climb (other than by boat) is to start at the top and

Distance: 127km *(79 miles)*
Elevation: 3,187m *(10,456ft)*

descend for 9.5km (6 miles). The gradient averages 7% and near the top the road performs an incredible 270-degree loop, twisting around and back under itself in an iconic hairpin called the 'tie knot'.

Mallorca has built quite a reputation for cycling, initially thanks to its popularity among professional riders. Sa Calobra has seen more than 100,000 climbs logged by 64,000 riders using the Strava app, and the island itself is said to host more than 40,000 cyclo-tourists every year.

This ride starts in the village of Caimari. You'll warm up on the quieter routes of the island as you head to Selva, which cuts through orange groves and up into the ridge ahead, through Lloseta to Alaró. Here, a café stop will prepare you for the ascent to Valldemossa.

This climb brings you gently into the mountain range that skirts the northern edge of the island. It's a mere 5km (3 miles) at 5%, but it sees the road turn from wide and busy into winding and narrow. The village at the top is dotted with the blonde stone houses set into the steep inclines of the valley that typify the Balearic Islands. You leave town via a corridor of tall trees and the road leads you towards the sea. By the time you approach the coastal village of Deià you've seen some of Mallorca's prettiest vistas (albeit at speed). Further down the coast you arrive >>

>> at the town of Sóller, from where you tackle the double whammy of the Puig Major and Sa Calobra.

The Puig Major – affectionately named The Pig – is the island's highest ascent, with a summit at 850m (2,789ft) and a total gain of 830m (2,723ft). It rolls up at an average of 6% over 13.7km (8½ miles), with a few harsh 10% ramps. As you gain height you'll catch glimpses of the valley below and the sea through gaps in the trees. When you near the summit, marked by a tunnel into the mountain, the view opens up to reveal a stunning mixture of thick forest, ragged limestone and sparkling blue sea. A sharp descent takes you around a limestone cliff overlooking a mountain reservoir and below a dilapidated aqueduct until you reach the bottom of the climb to the Coll dels Reis. Once you've climbed that comes the highlight of the day.

Sa Calobra (also known as The Snake) was built solely for tourism and was intended to be a thing of beauty as much as it was a means of access to a coastal town. The road was opened in 1932, and is still considered a masterpiece of modern construction.

With largely open views of the road ahead and a succession of dizzying hairpins, the descent feels like a go-kart track, with one inviting twist and turn after another. If you're here during the onset of evening, you'll have the road largely to yourself – enjoy it.

The Sa Calobra ascent that awaits you on the return leg is an almost perfect test of form. Taking around 35 minutes for a good amateur, it requires both power and endurance, and has long been a favourite of the UCI WorldTour pros. Just after 2km (1¼ miles) comes the first landmark – a pair of giant stone slabs that lean against each other like a perfectly balanced pair of cards – and soon you emerge from the trees of the lower slopes through a landscape of rock formations, with the road above spread over the hillside in a series of folds like a cloth draped over the landscape.

Over time this road has come to be known by cyclists simply as Sa Calobra

The tie knot comes into view with only 2km (1¼ miles) to go, and once you're there the sea and sun act in tandem to spotlight the mountain formations of the coast, all decorated by a perfect ribbon of road.

Ride back over the summit, through the stone arches, then follow the road on its sinewy descent from Lluc to Caimari. By now, if the sun is setting you should find you have the road to yourself, with only a few straggling cyclists and tourists making their way home in the last light of a day that will live long in the memory.

Western Europe

SWITZERLAND
Swiss Alps

With empty roads, leg-shredding climbs and pulse-quickening descents, this epic Swiss circuit should go straight to the top of your 'must-do rides' list.

Distance: 125km *(78 miles)*
Elevation: 4,547m *(14,918ft)*

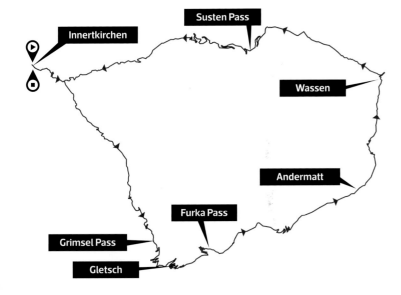

There aren't many places more glorious for riding a bike than the Swiss Alps in the summer. Nor are there many places more gruelling on the way up or rewarding on the way down. This is a ride, literally, from the heavens.

It is also a ride that doesn't require a great deal of navigational skill. You turn right in Innertkirchen to head up and over the Grimsel Pass, then left in Gletsch to head over the Furka Pass. In the valley you follow signs to Wassen, where you turn left onto the Susten Pass, which takes you all the way back to the start.

There isn't much time to warm creaking muscles before the tarmac tilts upwards, but at least it starts gently. Tunnels cut through the rock lower down the ascent, but a couple of times there is the option of taking the old road around the edge, which is rather fun, particularly as they're partly cobbled.

This road was dubbed the 'King of All Climbs' at the 2002 Tour de Suisse, and it's easy to see why. During the last few hairpins of the Grimsel, you may well find yourself stretching out a hand for the snow on the insides of the corners to cool yourself down. Yet, even in summer, as soon as you reach the top there's an instant need to put on extra layers.

The descent from the Grimsel Pass is disappointingly brief, and it feels like poor reward that just as you're getting into your stride around the huge switchbacks, the road reaches a junction where you have to begin climbing once more, to the highest point of the day. You can at least rattle along the first section of the Furka at a decent pace, admiring the way the road zigzags up the face opposite, the hairpins on concrete struts showcasing human and geological engineering in perfect harmony. But as the altimeter clicks over 2,000m (6,562ft), the road decides you need a double whammy of pain and ramps up the gradient to reduce all but the purest of climbers to a crawl.

On the descent you really are cycling through a filmset, because this side of the pass was used for the scene in *Goldfinger* where James Bond is chasing Tilly Masterson in his Aston Martin DB5. The first 5km (3 miles) or so are a little unnerving as there's no guardrail to offer even notional protection between you and the drops off the side of the road. At this altitude they really are big drops, and it's not a very friendly place to get it wrong, but after all the climbing it's a wonderful release to let the bike run.   >>

>> **With the village of Realp in sight, the gradient** lessens a fraction. From here the road runs straight and parallel to a railway line, and you can sustain a reasonable 45km/h (28mph) to eat up the distance. Before long, however, you're onto the final pass of the day, and the climb up the Susten Pass is 18km (11 miles) of gradual torture. Unlike the Grimsel, which, although longer, somehow hid the summit from view, you can clearly see the Susten stretching out endlessly in front of you. There are just two hairpins for relief and they only come near the end.

The road finally flattens out and your muscles ease for the first time in an hour and a half. At the entrance to the 300-m (328-yd) tunnel that marks the summit, there is a cathedral hush, in which the loudest noise is the gradually lessening pounding of your heart.

After a minute or two gazing at the view of the snowy, saw-toothed horizon, you'll want to turn around and freewheel through the unlit tunnel towards the stark white Alpine light on the other side. Within the first few corners of the descent, you're in cycling nirvana. The road is wide, like the descent from the Grimsel Pass, but its trajectory is more flowing. Near the top is a two-pronged waterfall, which, with the sun catching the spray, looks too perfect to be true.

There's hardly any need to turn the pedals more than just a few half rotations as the outside pedal switches from right to left between corners, and to accelerate into the odd sprint out of a hairpin to exercise tired hamstrings and keep them from cramping. Further down, the corners become more frequent and you need to continuously watch the vanishing point, trying to prejudge each bend's severity as it disappears around the rock face.

The entire run from tunnel to town takes nearly 40 glorious minutes, and you've covered a full 30km (18½ miles) of downhill by the time you come to a halt. It could well be the best and most spectacular descent you will ever ride.

This is a ride, literally, from the heavens

FRANCE

Secret Pyrenees

The Pyrenees in southern France may be a magnet for cyclists, but there are still beautiful, challenging corners of this mountain range where the crowds don't go.

There's something old-fashioned about cycling in the Midi-Pyrenees region of France. The rugged, rural terrain brings to mind those grainy black-and-white photographs of pioneering Tour de France cyclists panting over primitive mountain tracks to the cheers of local farmers.

The sparse and pastoral landscape provides a reminder that when the Tour first ventured into the Pyrenees, in 1910, the mountains weren't iconic emblems of achievement, but an unknown and wild terrain. The cruel gradients of the Tourmalet and other peaks are still there, and these legendary climbs remain a must for cycling aficionados. However, if you want a sense of what this region was like when the Tour first arrived, shift your attention eastwards to the 2,001-m (6,565-ft) Col de Pailhères and 1,680-m (5,512-ft) Col du Pradel. On their single-lane rural roads, with their sleepy villages and deserted valleys, you get a sense of isolation and an unexpected variety of terrain that resonate with the Tour's first forays into the Pyrenees.

This ride starts in Ax-les-Thermes, a small ski resort in the Ariège department of the Midi-Pyrenees, on a gentle rise eastwards along the D613. A right turn onto the D25 kicks off the 6–7% opening stretch from 715m (2,346ft) up to the Col de Pailhères at 2,001m (6,565ft). You skirt a mirrored lake at Goulours and follow the silver River Lauze, passing grey-green rockfaces on the left and dense forest on the right.

Ascending out of the morning mist reveals a spectacular panoramic view across the valley to the jagged mountains on the horizon. The climb is long at 19km (12 miles), but with fresh legs you can settle into a rhythm, occasionally getting out of the saddle to relieve chilled muscles. A sharp section of six switchbacks, peaking at a gradient of 10.5%, sees the altimeter leap upwards and you soon arrive at the Col de Pailhères.

This is not the place to be caught in a storm. Wooden signs have been bent sideways by years of high-altitude gusts, and the slither of road that zigzags down the mountain is fast and furious, even in clear weather, with gradients of up to 11.6%. There's no room for error on this tiny single-lane track, and by the time you reach the small riverside village of Mijanès at the bottom you'll have dropped 800m (2,625ft) in 10km (6 miles).

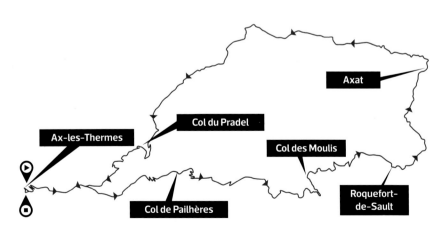

Axat

Col du Pradel

Ax-les-Thermes

Col des Moulis

Col de Pailhères

Roquefort-de-Sault

>>

Distance: 119km *(74 miles)*
Elevation: 3,288m *(10,787ft)*

The slither
of road that
zigzags down the
mountain is fast
and furious

>> Follow the D116 onto the D16, then cut left through the village of Le Pla to rejoin the D25 and glide up a short 100-m (328-ft) rise to the towns of Le Puch and Carcanières. Then there's a winding, guardrail-free descent into the valley, where you fly over an arched stone bridge across the River Aude into the village of Carcanières-les-Bains.

Following a sharp left onto the D17, you cross into the region of Languedoc, where the roads become rougher

and tighter as you climb the 1,099-m (3,606-ft) Col des Moulis and the 1,262-m (4,140-ft) Col du Garabeil, although with the gentle 6% gradients you can drink in the views of the forested valleys below. Then you continue through remote towns and past fields, orchards and pastures before diving through tunnels and under overhanging cliffs into the gorge below.

Arriving at the D118, you turn right and carve through the Aude Gorge along a road that runs parallel to the River Aude. Here is an opportunity

to pick up speed and enjoy the cool water that drips from the overhanging white cliffs.

Through the town of Axat, a left turn at the Pont d'Aliès takes you onto the D117 and D107 to the final leg-buster of the day, the 1,680-m (5,512-ft) Col du Pradel. The River Rébenty flows parallel to the road, and at the town of Joucou the sound of the current getting faster provides a warning that the gradient is about to rise to 9.7%.

This feels like another old-fashioned Pyrenean climb along a rough, spaghetti-thin track covered in mud and autumn leaves. Only the occasional clearing in the forest offers glimpses of the valley below as you ascend 1,000m (3,281ft) over 20km (12½ miles), but up ahead lies a mountain meadow framed by pine forests and mountains sprinkled with snow.

It's downhill all the way back to Ax-les-Thermes. The descent is terrifying. The road is a narrow, single-lane path covered in gravel and cow dung. Every switchback and blind corner demands precision as you drop 1,000m (3,281ft) in 15km (9⅓ miles) with gradients as steep as 9.6%. It feels like a video game as you clock up points for every obstacle dodged: potholes, cows and even the occasional passer-by. There won't be many of the latter, however, which is proof that, more than a century on from the Tour de France's first foray here, you can still find a patch in which to have your own unique Pyrenean adventure.

FRANCE
Roubaix

The cobbles of northern France offer up the most testing terrain in pro racing, and toughest of all are the brutal *pavé* sections of the Paris–Roubaix.

Cyclists are renowned for their pursuit of smoothness: a fluid pedal stroke, a well-executed shift or a perfectly rounded hairpin. We want pristine tarmac on which to ride a bike as the world glides by. And yet...

Paris–Roubaix is one of the great races. It's the Spring Classic that, along with the Tour of Flanders, every pro wants to win. Yet its infamous cobbles (*pavé*) are about as far away from smooth as you can get. The race isn't called the 'Hell of the North' for nothing, but it's also a rite of passage every cyclist should go through.

One other thing the cobbles are is accessible. From Lille, a principal crossroads for European high-speed trains, you head south to the village of Haveluy. This ride takes in 18 sections of *pavé* en route to the famous Roubaix Velodrome, where the race finishes. >>

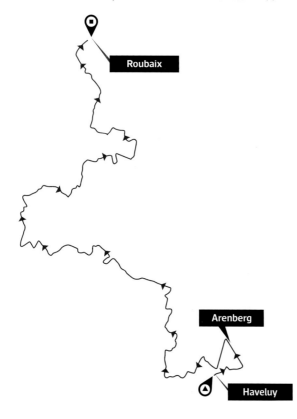

Roubaix

Arenberg

Haveluy

Distance: 106km *(66 miles)*
Elevation: 239m *(784ft)*

>> The ride starts with a gentle section to ease you in before taking in the second section of *pavé*, the Trouée d'Arenberg, which just happens to be the most fearsome of them all.

Cobbles are given star ratings, with five stars the toughest of them all. And this full-on, five-star stretch through the Arenberg forest is seen as Paris–Roubaix's first big test as the pros approach it in a headlong downhill rush at 60–70km/h (37–43mph). You probably won't be hitting that speed, but it will still feel too fast as the *pavé* looms. Some tips: try to hold the handlebars loosely and stay in the drops, not the hoods. Your arms and wrists are going to take a battering.

After the vast open horizons of northern France, it feels claustrophobic heading into the darkness of this foreboding corridor. And even though the 2.4-km (1½-mile) passage between the trees is arrow-straight, it also looks never-ending.

There's a barrier across the entrance to stop traffic, so you squeeze around it and then take to the cobbles. Instantly the bike takes on a life of its own. Aim for the pronounced crown of the road, where technically it's smoother, even if it's narrow and feels like cycling a lumpy tightrope. It can be hard to focus, too. Looking at the cobbles in front of the wheel can blur your vision at this distance, so you need to balance keeping an eye out for hazards with scanning the road ahead.

The bike will be jumping around wildly by the time you head under the iconic metal bridge that spans the cobbles like some industrial 'Welcome to Hell' banner. Try to relax, and stay in the biggest gear you can manage.

By the end of the 2,400m (7,874ft) you will feel a buzzing numbness in your hands from the vibrations, but there's a brief respite on a smooth road towards Pont Gibus, the next section. This has been given a four-star section, and although the cambers and subsidence are wild in places, it's easier and faster than Arenberg.

There's a bit more respite and then, just as the lactic acid is receding, you dive onto another stretch that's frequently covered in patches of thick, slimy mud. A group of cycling fans, Les Amis de Roubaix, look after the cobbles and repair the really badly damaged sections, but for most of the year the only groundsmen are the local farmers whose tractors and trailers shape the sections of *pavé*.

Next up is Mons-en-Pévèle, the second five-star sector. As you bounce around, trying to pick a line through the carnage, it's hard to imagine how the professionals cope as they jostle for position and hop around to hold a wheel or avoid a crash, all the while going faster than you can imagine. Some of the roads from here on in are even rougher than the Arenberg, as the ride continues its strange mixture of rural French serenity and cobbled brutality.

The last five-star section is the Carrefour de l'Arbre. There's absolutely no place to hide on its bleak long straights through featureless fields – until, that is, you reach the famous lonely bar at the end.

That's not the end of the ride, though. There's one final bit of *pavé* before the run into Roubaix down the long, straight avenue towards the Velodrome. It's a fantastic finale, the boards blissfully smooth as you roll down the banking and sprint for the line.

If you're a serious rider you really should experience some muddy, scary, violent, ancient farm tracks in northern France. There's even a beer in it for you if you head back to the bar.

FRANCE
Alpe d'Huez

This ride is on every serious rider's must-do list, but head into the rocky back country beyond the iconic Alpe d'Huez and you will find a little-known treasure trove of roads.

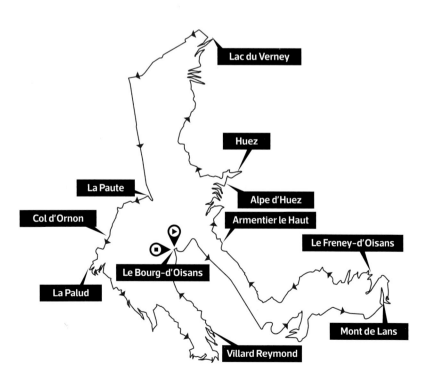

Alpe d'Huez is a giant of the Tour de France, a climb that was first used in 1952. Since then, it has been the site of a host of iconic moments: Fausto Coppi's famous attack on his way to victory on that first visit; Bernard Hinault and Greg LeMond crossing the line arm in arm in 1986; Marco Pantani's sensational record time in 1997. Oh, and in 2018 Geraint Thomas became the first rider to win the stage while wearing the Tour leader's yellow jersey, having gained the jersey by winning the previous stage.

The ascent is also famous for the fanatical supporters who line the stage, but you will need

Distance: 91km (56½ *miles*)
Elevation: 2,814m (*9,232ft*)

to make an early start to this route. It's unlikely you will have much in the way of company when you set off from the town of Le Bourg-d'Oisans, the modest capital of a magnificent Alpine valley in the heart of the Dauphiné region, unless, of course, you are here in July. In summer, cycling fans pack the town. (In winter, the town is full of skiers.) Depending on the weather, the cycling season runs from late April until mid-October. This region abounds with famous climbs, which form the walls of 'Fortress Oisans', including the Cols du Galibier, Télégraphe, Lautaret and Glandon and the Col de la Croix de Fer. But this route follows some of the lesser-known roads in the

area, so there are two things to note before we start. First, there are some sections of rough road so you need good tyres, ideally 25mm ones. Also, you will need to have lights – a legal requirement in France – because you will be riding through tunnels.

And we're off. From Le Bourg-d'Oisans, follow the Romanche upstream along the RN91, the main road through the valley to Briançon and Italy. The gradient is gentle and, in the early morning, the air crisp.

A few kilometres from Bourg you turn into the Gorges de l'Infernet and, still hugging the river, ride through the tunnel of the Rampe des Commères. That's the warm-up done. Turning away from the >>

>> river, you climb the old road to the ski resort of Les Deux Alpes, a beautiful route that switches back and forth through the dappled sunlight of a beech wood before emerging into mountain meadows.

In places, the corniche road edges dramatically along a shelf cut through bare rock. Then, from the hamlet of Bons and its glorious views across the valley to the saw-toothed, white-capped peaks of the Grandes Rousses massif, you plunge back down to the river and the village of Le Freney-d'Oisans before starting to climb again.

Sections of 13% gradient on the switchbacks make this a hard ascent and the steepest of the day. Eventually you reach the 'Balcon Road', essentially a cart track covered in tarmac, cut like a shelf and carved out of the rock in places, edging high along the valley wall with a precipitous drop over the side. As if that weren't enough, the road then heads downhill around a series of blind corners.

Soon you reach the road that climbs up to Alpe d'Huez. It's steep, of course, but this route only takes in 11 of the 21 famous hairpins before peeling off at the old village of Huez. From Huez you skirt the mountain to the sound of cowbells on a delightful road called Pas de la Confession. The road hugs the cliffs on the way to another pretty village, Villard Reculas. Ticking off the major climbs is fine, of course, and you can do that, too, but these smaller, quieter roads arguably have even more to offer.

Then you roar down past Lac du Verney to the valley floor and follow the main road for a few kilometres back towards Bourg to begin the final climb, a hefty 14km (9 miles) of ascent with 900m (2,953ft) of vertical gain. The ascent starts on the road to Col d'Ornon, the southwestern gateway out of 'Fortress Oisans' into Provence, beside the River Lignarre, with skyscraper mountains leaning in on both sides. Then, in La Palud, you turn left and cross the river to reach an even quieter, single-lane road.

Alpe d'Huez is a giant of the Tour de France

After edging up through a beech wood, the road enters a sweet-smelling forest of pines. An hour later, it emerges into a classic Alpine scene. Here, wildflower meadows create a polka-dot pattern of green, white, purple and orange, with the hamlet of Villard Reymond postcard-perfect in its bowl beneath the col.

From the col, at 1,626m (5,335ft), you can take the road via Villard Notre Dame – a technical, 11-km (7-mile) descent with plenty of switchbacks near the top and four long tunnels at the bottom. Or you could ride down the way you came up, as either route heads back to Bourg. Both are sensational descents that, at times, feel as if they're never going to end. If only.

Distance: **97km** *(60 miles)*
Elevation: **1,919m** *(6,296ft)*

FRANCE
Nice

The hills near Nice in southern France are a playground for the rich and famous, not to mention a host of professional riders racing to the sun.

There's Paris, and then there's Nice, the second most popular tourist city in France. Squashed onto only a few kilometres of Côte d'Azur coastline, Nice nestles between the celebrity hangouts of Cannes to the west and Monaco to the east. In summer the wealthy come to relax in their mansions, which lie empty for much of the rest of the year. The relaxed pace of the city means it's also a haven for professional cyclists, who gather to sip coffees in the local cafés before taking to the nearby hills to train. Riding here is like having a kickabout at the Bernabéu.

This loop out of Nice and around some of the region's best climbs begins in the city's bustling market quarter. You start by heading out of town on the road up the Col d'Èze, which winds its way upwards at an average gradient of 6% for around 10km (6 miles), with the occasional 10% spike. The ascent regularly features in the final stage of Paris–Nice, the UCI World Tour event nicknamed 'The Race to the Sun' for its position on the calendar. As well as being

the first big European race of the season every March, it is unique in that the route takes riders across wintry mountains to the warmth of the coast.

While some climbs can be a slog from start to finish, Col d'Èze has a slightly gentler profile, and once the gradient slackens you can stretch your legs and take in the views over Nice and the coastline. If you have to start a ride with a big climb, there can't be many better, and as the sea steadily drops further away to your right, more and more opulent homes start to appear. There's a distinct absence of traffic, and the fresh seaside air mixes with a herbal scent. Then there's another faint smell in the air, which becomes more acute as you approach the outskirts of Monaco. It's the whiff of money.

The tax haven looks quite ridiculous from above. Crammed into just 200 hectares (about 500 acres), Monaco may be spotlessly clean and awash with billionaires, but the architecture is bland and functional. Nondescript high-rises crowd the hilly >>

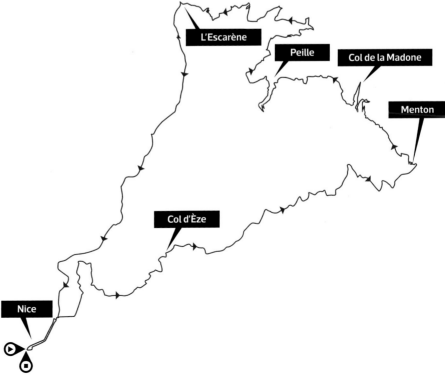

>> coastline in what is the world's most densely populated country, a place that a number of the better-paid pro cyclists and many other sportsmen call home.

Don't worry, you don't need to access your bank account here because you skirt past the maze-like mayhem of casinos and gin palaces to head straight for Menton, a much more genteel spot further down the coast, before the day's main event: the Col de la Madone. Thanks to Trek's Madone bike, this is probably the most famous climb never to have featured in the Tour de France, but the Madone is a perfect training ground for the professionals. At 13km (8 miles) long and averaging around 7%, it begins almost at sea level before rearing up to an altitude of 925m (3,035ft). The initial stretches out of Menton look quite scruffy, but the scenery quickly gets a lot prettier, and the aroma of pine soon fills your nostrils.

The road weaves under the viaduct that carries the main Franco–Italian autoroute. As you pass the giant pillars for the second time it feels like you're really back in the sticks and scaling a proper Alpine ascent. The houses look more normal, too. There's a sense of life being lived up here, rather than the little-used splendour of the holiday district nearby.

The view back towards where you started is utterly magnificent as you wind your way up to Sainte-Agnès, but beyond the village the road cuts back on itself and becomes narrower and rougher. A couple of short, unlit tunnels mean you're near the top, and then it's a sweeping descent to the old village of Peille, which is an ideal spot to take a break for lunch.

From here you head on the back roads to L'Escarène along a meandering, gravelly lane that hugs the contours of a large valley. Every now and then a grate for run-off water crosses your path. Play close attention here. If your front wheel lodges in one, you'll be over the handlebars and seeing stars of a different kind to the ones who populate the apartments of Monte Carlo.

Finally, from L'Escarène you head onto the quicker, wider D2204 to zip back down to Nice, and for the final 20km (12½ miles) it feels as if you hardly have to turn the pedals. By now it will have struck you how you're getting a taste of what it's like to be a pro, and there's a good chance you will have spotted some of them training along the way if you've timed your trip right. The big difference is that you once you arrive back in Nice, you can enjoy dinner without having to count the calories. Cheers!

ANDORRA – FRANCE – SPAIN
Three in one

If you get your planning right, you can visit three countries
in one ride and discover a different climate
and riding culture in each.

Andorra is an unusual cycling playground. A landlocked principality in the eastern Pyrenees, it's the sixth-smallest country in Europe, with a population of just 85,000. Yet its high-altitude peaks make great fodder for cyclists. The average elevation of the country is a lung-popping 1,996m (6,548ft), and both the Tour de France and Vuelta a España have ventured here for the high altitudes and mountainous terrain.

This route starts with a short, punchy climb out of the ski resort of El Pas de la Casa to the 2,408-m (7,900-ft) Port d'Envalira. Unpredictable weather is one of Andorra's many unique charms and this is the highest paved road in the Pyrenees, so mounds of snow may be piled up by the sides of the tarmac

even in summer. Thick fog is also common on this pass so you may find you're cycling through clouds of cotton wool. It can be a harsh environment but is an atmospheric place to ride a bike.

When you round the summit, any fog clears to replace a monochrome world with an incredible view of the valley below. Ahead of you is a patchwork of dark meadows and thick pine forests surrounded by snow-dusted mountains. More than 90 per cent of the Andorran landscape is forest. And the grey sliver of tarmac snaking downhill feels like an invitation, as does the snug-looking valley below.

The tarmac is as rough as sandpaper and offers plenty of grip, allowing you to descend at pace. Giant boulders dumped by landslides lie by the side of the road, while some of the more precarious rock faces are held back by giant metal nets. The road curls in a wide arch around the village of El Tarter before a long, straight stretch of descent allows you to gather even more speed. The expansive views eventually close in when you arrive in Encamp, which is nestled in the valley at an altitude of 1,267m (4,157ft). The forests, gorges and steep cliffs give this region a more claustrophobic feel, but the warmer temperatures are welcome after a chilly descent.

The next stop is the capital, Andorra la Vella, an odd mix of old stone streets, modern bridges, Romanesque churches and glass-fronted buildings. After another 8km (5 miles) of descent from here, you will encounter the black booths of the border crossing into Spain. Cyclists are waved straight through into the   >>

El Tarter

Col de Puymorens

FRANCE

Port d'Envalira

El Pas de la Casa

Andorra la Vella   ANDORRA

Puigcerdà

CATALONIA

La Seu d'Urgell

Distance: 137km *(85 miles)*
Elevation: 2,048m *(6,719ft)*

It can be a harsh environment but is an atmospheric place to ride a bike

>> autonomous region of Catalonia, and immediately it feels different. The valley is humid and the jagged peaks of Andorra have been replaced by a dry, dusty, Mediterranean landscape.

The long, flat roads in Catalonia are perfect for riding hard and offer the opportunity for doing some time-trial training. You will now ride for around an hour past fields of wheat, stone farmhouses, Roman ruins, ochre cliffs and barren scrubland. The next leg, from the town of La Seu d'Urgell to Puigcerdà, near

the border with France, involves a slow, steady ascent of more than 500m (1,640ft). It can be made more pleasant by a detour to the town of Ger for a lunch stop before you turn left out of Catalonia and head over the border with France.

The final major challenge is a 25-km (15½-mile) ascent to Col de Puymorens in the French Pyrenees, and the terrain soon changes for the third time on this ride. The sharper and more rugged Pyrenean

landscape is filled with rocky mountains, dense forests and stone walls. The weather is likely to change, too, with grey clouds draining the colour from the sky and wind whipping through the valley. If the Alps are the heartland of Europe, then the Pyrenees are the border badlands. It is a wild region and locals have historically been subjected to a very basic and arduous rural existence.

An old railway line runs parallel to the road, serving as a reminder of those early Tour de France cheats who used to jump on the train to save time, which doesn't seem such a bad idea as you grind up the climb. When you reach Porté-Puymorens, at an altitude of 1,640m (5,380ft), a tunnel diverts any vehicles, leaving you completely alone on the mountain road up to the pass of the 1,920-m (6,299-ft) Col de Puymorens. Here a series of switchbacks guides you into the clouds. All around you is a magnificent canvas of folded grey mountains and forests of pine, beech and fir. This is the sort of cruel but beautiful Pyrenean landscape that has seduced and terrified cyclists for years.

Past the summit there's a final kick up towards your starting point back in Andorra at El Pas de la Casa, at 2,080m (6,824ft). You've visited three countries and, if the weather is against you, you'll finish your ride with yet another treble: you won't be able to feel your cheeks, your hands or your toes. But it will all have been worthwhile.

BELGIUM
Flanders

The hills of Flanders hold a gruesome appeal for anyone familiar with the lore of the Cobbled Classics. Just be sure to attack them at full tilt.

I t seems only fair to warn you that you don't go cycling in Flanders for the scenery. But Flanders is much more fun than that. Mountain passes can be conquered with compact gearsets, but no amount of sprocket switching will make the cobbled climbs in this part of Belgium any easier. You come here precisely because it's hard and unique.

This route starts in Oudenaarde, opposite the Tour of Flanders museum in the centre of the town, with a ride out to the trees and the first climb of the day. The 2.2-km (1⅓-mile) Oude Kwaremont starts going uphill while still on tarmac, but you can see the cobbles ahead and there's no point trying to soften the blow. It's better to attack with purpose, so hold your hands on the horizontal section of the handlebars, relax your grip and keep your legs pushing hard in as big a gear as you think you can sustain.   >>

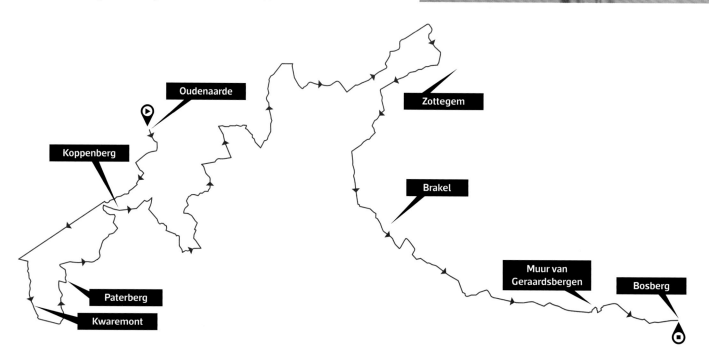

Oudenaarde

Zottegem

Koppenberg

Brakel

Paterberg

Muur van Geraardsbergen

Bosberg

Kwaremont

Distance: **91km** *(57 miles)*
Elevation: **1,049m** *(3,442ft)*

>> The violence of the first few metres is still such a juddering shock that it's difficult to remember to keep pedalling. The vibrations hit your arms like rapid-fire recoils from ammunition. Your legs are fresh, though, and speed is your friend because if you can go fast enough you get this wonderful sensation of skimming over the top of the stones.

The steepest bit of the Kwaremont is only about 600m (656yd) long, at an average gradient of around 7%, but it comes at the beginning and if you drain too much energy you'll suffer on the kilometre (²/₃ mile) of false flat that follows. At the top there's a sharp right onto the main road, where you turn left and your vision stabilizes on a wide stretch of road that plunges downhill and then up again straightaway.

Turn off the main road again and descend a winding single track towards the Paterberg, which starts at a 90-degree right-hander. If the Kwaremont's relatively gentle gradient lulls you into a false sense of security, the Paterberg shatters it immediately. It towers over you like some huge tsunami of cobbles, and you have no option but to drop to the small ring on the front as the initial 16% gradient kicks in. The whole climb is only about 400m (1,312ft), but with an average of 14% and a middle section of over 20% it's brutal for both your lungs and your legs.

When you turn left at the top, there's some respite before the most fearsome climb of the day. It's not often that you see professionals walking up hills, but every year they do exactly that on the Koppenberg. The most treacherous section is halfway up – 300m (984ft) in – at 22%, with root-strewn earth banks crowding in on either side. At times it feels like mountain biking up a technical rocky climb as you navigate between the yawning gaps and the worst of the cobbles.

Next up is Steenbeekdries, a Roubaix-style section of *pavé* with a slight incline, before a fast, straight descent towards the Taaienberg ('tough mountain'). Here you can use the smooth gutter at the side of the road to tackle the maximum 18% gradient.

Now comes the curiously suburban Eikenberg, which is followed by another stretch of *pavé* (the Marterstraat) en route to the Molenberg. This funnels you across a narrow bridge before unceremoniously spitting you onto rough cobbles beneath the trees as you climb steeply around a right-hander.

Once you've then tackled the strength-sapping section of *pavé* called the Paddestraat, there are just two more cobbled climbs to go. Unfortunately there are two un-cobbled climbs standing in the way. The first is the Tenbosse, a fairly wide street on the outskirts of Brakel. The second is the Kapelmuur, or Muur van Geraardsbergen, which used to be the penultimate climb and frequently the decisive point of the Tour of Flanders.

Eventually the concrete gives way to tarmac as you descend into the Geraardsbergen and along the high street, but before you know it the cobbles have arrived, stretching out for the best part of a kilometre (²/₃ mile) to the climb's 20% denouement up near the golden-topped chapel. You wind around the church before turning away from the traffic into the trees to the right.

Here in the darkness the road ramps up to 20% on cobbles that form an almost serrated surface. There's a false flat, then you burst back into the light as the cobbles kick up once more into their famous snaking flourish.

A sweeping downhill is your reward for all the climbing effort, and then finally there's the Bosberg, a long drag on asphalt that nibbles at your reserves and stops you rushing the 10% cobbled section through the trees. You will feel a flood of relief at the top and you wouldn't care about a view even if there were one.

FRANCE
Col d'Izoard

At 2,360m (7,743ft), the Izoard is regularly a literal Tour de France high point, and it has been the scene of many an epic ride. And you, too, can tackle this true classic.

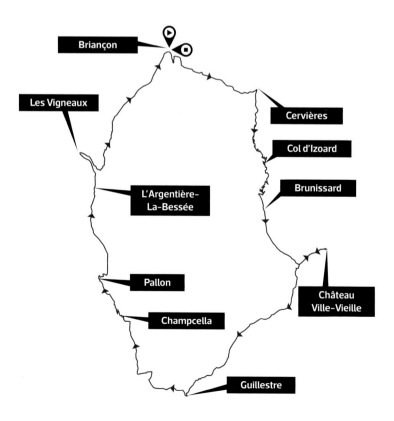

Briançon

Les Vigneaux

Cervières

Col d'Izoard

L'Argentière-La-Bessée

Brunissard

Pallon

Champcella

Château Ville-Vieille

Guillestre

'**A** new version of hell' is how Jacques Goddet, director of the Tour de France between 1936 and 1986, described the otherworldly terrain of the Col d'Izoard. In his eyes, the mountain represented 'this terrible exigency which establishes the border of the difficult and the terrifying'.

The Izoard is unique for its strange rock pinnacles at the top, along with its quiet roads and warm, early-summer climate. A giant of the Tour, the climb has traditionally been tackled from the south in a brutal 16-km (10-mile), 1,095-m (3,592-ft) ascent from the town of Guillestre,

Distance: 98km (61½ *miles*)
Elevation: 2,194m (7,198ft)

with an average gradient of 6.9% and cruel kicks of 14%. This route tackles it in the opposite direction from Briançon in the north, as used in the 2017 Tour. It forms part of a 98-km (61-mile) loop, and from this side the climb is 20km (12½ miles) in length, with a 1,141-m (3,743-ft) elevation gain and an average gradient of 5.7%, albeit with prolonged sections at 8–9%.

Starting in the fortified mountain town of Briançon, head east along the D902 up and over the Col. Initially the gradient rises to 7% before mellowing to a 3–4% gradient en route to the village of Cervières, where you swing south. The road slyly creeps up to 7%, and soon all you can see of Cervières are the slanted grey

roofs of its chalets. Continuing into a forest of pine and larch, you will tackle 16 hairpins in 3km (2 miles), a couple of which rise above 15% and will have you out of the saddle for the first time.

Even in summer you're likely to find the road lined with dense slabs of ice, and eventually you will emerge from the trees into a vast white valley surrounded by stately mountains. Ahead is the Refuge Napoléon – built by the man himself in 1858 – which marks the final 200-m (219-yd) dash to the top.

Only when you round the summit and enter into the Parc Naturel Régional du Queyras does the >>

>> valley on the southern side reveal itself. It is a stark, unforgiving landscape of wind-blasted scree slopes and craggy cliffs drizzled in snow, with thick forests nestled far below. After around 100m (328ft) of vertical descent, you reach the eerie world of the Casse Déserte ('Broken Desert'), where strange pinnacles of rock, which shift colour throughout the day, jut out of the earth like fangs, and loose stones plummet down the ridges.

Just before the hamlet of La Draye, there's a cluster of 12 switchbacks, and then there's a long, straight dash through the hamlets of Brunissard, La Chalp and Le Coin. If the smell of freshly baked bread in the village of Arvieux makes you hungry, it's worth taking a short detour at the 43km (27 miles) to Château Ville-Vieille, a picturesque village beneath the 13th-century Fort Queyras, for lunch. Then continue south through the valley for 20km (12½ miles).

The road traces the path of the River Guil, where the valley is long and straight enough to reveal glimpses of distant white peaks on the horizon. Here you will come upon a series of tunnels, whose cool shade provides a welcome break from the sunshine. Where the road passes vertiginous drops, the sides are lined with stone barriers like rows of giant molars.

Arriving in Guillestre, which at 900m (2,953ft) in altitude is the lowest point of the route, you turn right onto the D902A. This western side of the clockwise loop is in stark contrast to the sparkling snows of the Izoard and the epic terrain of the Queyras Valley. Here the environment is more bucolic, with narrow roads, quaint villages, old churches and sleepy campsites.

Now 80km (50 miles) into the ride, turn right at Chanteloube for a punchy 3-km (2-mile) climb that averages 7–8%, with bends that ramp up to 15%. Here you can see the tributaries of the River Durance, which spread like tentacles across the open plain, and the dense chain of mountains that guard the opposite

Even in summer you're likely to find the road lined with dense slabs of ice

side of the valley. From the top there's a gentle descent before you turn right at Pallon, dropping further along the Champ du Seigneur before joining the D138A just west of La Roche-de-Rame. Following a short ride along the west side of the Durance, there's a final 360-m (1,181-ft) climb to Villard Meyer. The ascent has an average gradient of 4–5%, with a few short sections at 9–12%, but here you can empty the tank before joining the N94 back to Briançon.

Having hurtled down the south side of the Izoard at 70km/h (43mph), you will understand how climbing the mountain in the opposite direction inspired Tour de France founder Henri Desgrange to declare, 'The Izoard is unnerving, like a story that will keep you up all night and which lasts forever.' Tackled in the opposite direction it will be the memories, not the pain, that endure.

Distance: 149km *(93 miles)*
Elevation: 3,900m *(12,795ft)*

FRANCE
Central Pyrenees

The Pyrenees have more than their fair share of classic climbs, and on this ride you'll take a stab at four of them in quick succession.

Conditions have improved considerably since the Tour de France's first visit to the Pyrenees in 1910, when third-placed finisher Gustave Garrigou voiced his fears about 'avalanches, road collapses, killer mountains and the thunder of God'. Yet this remains a wild and inhospitable region, which is precisely what draws cyclists to the epic climbs that have graced the world's most monumental bicycle race. And tackling three of them in one day – with one more gruelling ascent, which not even the Tour has tackled, thrown in for good measure – sounds like a challenge too good to ignore.

This ride starts in the village of Bertren and takes in four leg-shredding Pyrenean beasts: Port de Balès, the Col de Peyresourde, Superbagnères and an uncategorized ascent to the Hospice de France.

The climb to Port de Balès starts at Mauléon-Barousse and threads its way up a narrow, twisting gorge before emerging onto a luminous green carpet of pastureland 17km (10½ miles) later. The road is pinched close in places, hemmed in by a rock wall on one side and a seemingly fathomless, tree-cluttered drop on the other. The gradient averages nearly 8% but occasionally twitches up to almost double that without warning, and it's the jolting shifts in gradient that make the Pyrenees so hard. The key here is to preserve as much energy as you can for later on.

Eventually you emerge above the treeline and into a bowl of pastureland. The sense of isolation is inescapable, especially at the summit. There's nothing up here, just a sign announcing your height – 1,755m (5,758ft) – and a wind that cuts like a knife. Don some extra layers and head over the other side as the road unfurls in a long, lazy wriggle down the length of the valley. You'll encounter two tight hairpins about halfway down, and there will be a sheer drop to the valley floor on your right for most of the way. At Mayrègne you turn right and immediately start heading uphill on the climb to the Col de Peyresourde. It's in stark contrast to the claustrophobic Port de   >>

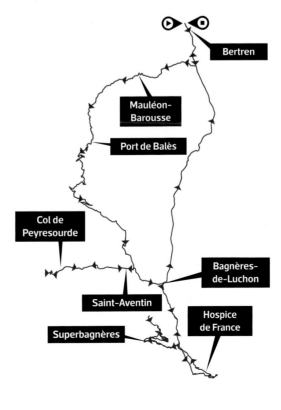

Bertren

Mauléon-Barousse

Port de Balès

Col de Peyresourde

Bagnères-de-Luchon

Saint-Aventin

Hospice de France

Superbagnères

>> Balès, offering wide-open views across rolling pastures to snowcapped peaks. The road is smooth and spacious but will keep you on your toes with a gradient that fluctuates between 6% and 11%. The final few kilometres are marked by a series of hairpins with views back down the valley, which looks like a carpet of moss. Even better than the view is the fact that there is a hut dispensing omelettes, frites and crêpes at the 1,569-m (5,148-ft) summit.

The ride back down the same road is completely different to the ascent. Once beyond the hairpins, the road is basically straight for the rest of the descent into Luchon, and you can pick up some serious speed.

Next up from here is the third, and biggest, climb of the day, at just over 19km (12 miles), with a gain in elevation of 1,200m (3,937ft), to the ski station of Superbagnères. Once past the turn-off for the Hospice de France, which you'll be revisiting soon enough, the road crosses a bridge and you start a merciless grind that seems to go on for ever, with the toughest section the final set of hairpins at an average of 9%. Between breaks in the trees, the views to the distant, cloud-wreathed peaks are impressive, but the summit itself is unlike any other and feels slightly eerie. All that's there to greet you are the haunted, skeletal remains of the Grand Hotel, an out-of-season ski resort. The hotel's ornate 1920s facade lives up to its name but is strangely at odds with its mountaintop eyrie.

From Superbagnères, today's final test is the 6-km (3¾-mile) climb to Hospice de France up a narrow, twisting road that leads to the site of a 14th-century shelter for religious pilgrims. Although this is the only ascent of the day not to have featured in the Tour, that doesn't mean it's easy. By this point your legs will be creaking to a virtual standstill on the first of several 16% ramps. Each succeeding ramp disappears behind a wall of trees, and there are no roadside signs so you have no idea how far there is to go. Eventually, the climb's only hairpin offers the briefest breather, and soon you'll see, painted on the road, '300m'...'200m'...'100m'. Under a canopy of trees the road flattens out and there's a sign that finally, joyously, announces 'Hospice de France'.

It's effectively all downhill going back to Bertren, although you may well encounter a block headwind in the valley all the way. And if you fancy a glass of wine when you're back in the warm, you may also find that you're too exhausted even to raise the glass to your lips. It's that sort of ride.

SWITZERLAND

Davos

When it's not hosting global political leaders, Davos in Switzerland makes the ideal starting point for this stunning ride that tackles two spectacularly contrasting climbs.

Distance: 114km *(71 miles)*
Elevation: 2,800m *(9,186ft)*

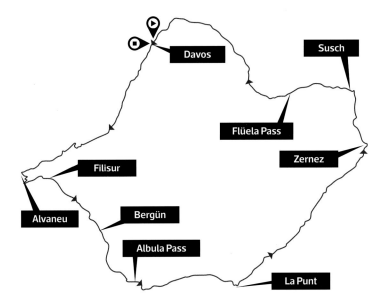

Compared with the picture-postcard scenery of the Albula Pass, the nearby Flüela Pass is its no-nonsense, get-to-the-point cousin. It's not ugly exactly, but it's more Mickey Rourke than Johnny Depp – rugged, uncompromising and not an encounter you're likely to forget in a hurry.

The Albula Pass and the Flüela Pass are barely 20km (12½ miles) apart, and both rise to over 2,300m (7,546ft) in a far-flung corner of Switzerland famous for winter sports and celebrity visitors. Halfway up the first, electric trains crisscross fast-flowing rivers on 100-year-old stone viaducts. Halfway up the second, a distant glacier glints in the late afternoon sunshine. They are linked by the Engadin Valley, where forests of fir and larch trees look down upon a raging river, pencil-thin clock towers and cobbled town squares.

The ride starts in Davos, at 1,560m (5,118ft) above sea level the highest city in Europe and home to the annual World Economic Forum. You head south on the fast, wide Funtauna Road, which follows a railway line and river down into the Landwasser Valley. It's an easy, exhilarating warm-up that takes you into the 2.7-km (1⅔-mile) Landwasser Tunnel (well illuminated, unlike many of its French and Italian counterparts) and through pretty villages full of flower-bedecked balconies and pastel-coloured shutters.

For the next 20km (12½ miles) you can stretch your legs and gulp down pure Alpine air. You pass through Wiesen and Alvaneu, then turn left onto a well-surfaced but narrow lane that plunges steeply down to the railway and river before starting its almost imperceptible climb towards the Albula Pass.

By the time the valley walls close in on you, the gradient has asserted itself and you'll be out of the saddle. Another river crashes through the gorge to your right, until its roaring subsides as the road snakes upwards towards a distant chink in the wall of rock above us. Once you're through this gap, a whole new panorama of rolling pastures, dense forests and rugged peaks is revealed, and in the middle of this natural amphitheatre is the village of Bergün. Here the road surface turns to cobbles and slants upwards through a warren of stone and timber buildings.

The road continues up with its ever-present watery companion tumbling alongside it in the opposite direction. You're rejoined by the Swiss mountain railway, and by a feat of engineering so daring that it's listed as a UNESCO World Heritage Site. It's a series of soaring stone viaducts and curving tunnels that allow the >>

>> railway to defeat the mountain's gradient by spiralling upwards in 360-degree circles like a corkscrew.

At Preda the road flattens briefly as the railway vanishes into a tunnel, then continues for another 10km (6 miles) to the pass. Here, finally, the road flattens out and threads its way past lakes and through wildflower meadows. A succession of steep hairpins takes you down to the valley floor and the town of La Punt. Turn left here and follow the River Inn as it courses through one pretty village after another.

By the time you arrive in Susch, the valley has been reduced to a narrow strip hemmed in by soaring sentinels of rock. Disconcertingly, the steep rock face blotting out the sky to your left appears to have a road zigzagging up it. This is the start of the climb, an abrupt jolt to the senses and digestive system as the road rears up in a succession of 10% and 12% ramps. The Flüela Pass goes on for 15km (9 miles), with a vertical climb of 900m (2,953ft). At one point there isn't enough mountainside to accommodate the curve and gradient of the road, so those dastardly Swiss engineers have built what is effectively a horseshoe-shaped motorway flyover in the middle of the Alpine forest.

After these initial steep switchbacks, the road straightens and wriggles off up the side of the mountain for as far as the eye can see. Its gradient is manageable and constant, at least. There's a deepening valley to your left, and a patch of white glinting in the distance. This is the glacier known as Vadret da Grialetsch. Just when you think it's within touching distance, you veer right into another sequence of steep hairpins and up into a new valley, even more desolate than the last. You'll know you're near the top when the dense forests give way to bare rock and threadbare patches of grass. The road twists back and forth and the wind is unrelenting, but finally you reach the hut that marks the summit.

It's a long plunge back to Davos, and the final few kilometres take you past a golf course, luxury hotels, a convention centre that has been graced by presidents and prime ministers, and a branch of Aldi. The contrast between opulence and thrift is as striking as that between the mountain passes you have just conquered.

Electric trains crisscross fast flowing rivers

Distance: 142km *(88 miles)*
Elevation: 3,683m *(12,083ft)*

FRANCE
Vercors

With its towering cliffs, precarious hanging roads and stunning scenery, the Vercors region of France should be teeming with riders. *Should* be.

They call it the Fortress, and you will understand why when you see the forbidding cliff faces of the Vercors Massif. Yellow-grey limestone rock intermingles with swathes of luscious green vegetation, pouring into gorges and spilling through valleys to create a truly unique, and slightly daunting, citadel.

Few people know it's here, though, because there are the Alps on one side and Mont Ventoux on the other. But what the area lacks in snowy peaks, it makes up for in mysterious tunnel passages, cliff-hanging roads and a welcome lack of tourists. It's an undiscovered gem.

This loop of the massif starts in Saint-Jean-en-Royans, from which you take the D54 north to skirt the western flank of the plateau. You head through shady walnut groves and over bridges spanning the streams that make their way first to the River Isère and then on to the mighty Rhône.

In the town of Pont-en-Royans, in which every building appears to be perilously stuck to a cliff, you cross the River Bourne and get your first glimpse into the daunting massif interior through a gap in the cliff. Then you roll into the village of Cognin-les-Gorges and follow signs for the Gorges du Nan. The first buttresses of the plateau erupt out of the ground in a wall of vegetation. Nonetheless, the road manages to find an opening in the forest and picks its way back and forth up the face of the cliff.

The easy pace of the opening 30km (19 miles) is quickly forgotten at this point, although after only a few switchbacks the road seemingly comes to an abrupt halt, as if blocked by a landslide. Fear not. Once you reach the apparent blockade, the road turns 90-degree to funnel into a tiny hole in the adjacent cliff, and a tunnel so low you'll stoop almost without thinking. This 30-m (33-yd) stretch of darkness is like a portal to a new world, and you emerge like the children of Narnia into the heart of the Gorges du Nan. 　　>>

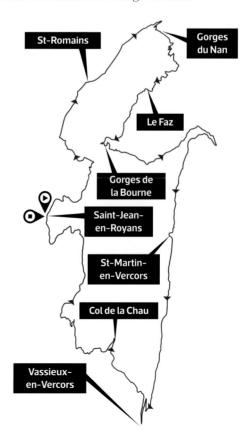

>> The road has been carved into the side of the cliff, and all that separates it from the perilous drop to the right is a very low wall. The views past the interlocking spurs of limestone cliffs and dense forests to the edge of the plateau high above are stunning, but you'll need to get your head down over the following 12km (7½ miles) of climbing to reach the Coulmes Plateau.

On exiting the gorge, the landscape becomes more expansive, although the top of the plateau is covered with forest until you round a corner and are transported into yet another world – that of Gorges de la Bourne. It's different from the tight, ravine-like Gorges du Nan. The view stretches into the distance, the sea of flora broken only by a series of limestone monoliths.

Once you reach the bottom, you turn left and head east up the valley, tracing the River Bourne all the way to the top. Once you're between the cliffs, it's like navigating the passages of a gigantic termite mound. From the summit, turn south and make your way across the valleys of the Drôme, where La Chapelle-en-Vercors makes an ideal stop-off point.

Despite having made your way onto the plateau, the road is still sneaking upwards in an undulating fashion as you skip between valleys and cross over streams. The southernmost point of the ride takes you past a deserted ski station and through a tunnel to the top of the Col de Rousset, a 20-km (12½-mile) climb that winds its way up to the plateau from the town of Die. Then you whizz down the other side before dropping into Vassieux-en-Vercors to enter the final third of the loop, clawing your way back out of the basin to the highest point of the ride, the Col de la Chau, at 1,337m (4,386ft).

From here it's downhill all the way home, and as you descend you enter the Fôret de Lente – a 3,000-hectare (7,413-acre) wilderness of wolves, wild boar, wild sheep and deer – before rounding a corner to be confronted by the Combe Laval. Cutting almost 4km (2½ miles) into the plateau interior, the gorge's grandeur is accentuated by the perilous vertical cliffs that surround it. The climb you're about to descend is 13km (8 miles) back to Saint-Jean-en-Royans, and its summit perches almost 900m (2,953ft) above the valley floor. The road trickles off to your left through a tunnel before re-emerging further down from a vertiginous hole in the cliff, with sheer faces above and below.

While coasting your way back to base, in and out of tunnels on a narrow shelf of road looking out across the abyss, the scenes are spectacular. Your victory at the Fortress is complete. It's time to beat a retreat.

FRANCE

Col de la Croix de Fer

The infamous Col de la Croix de Fer is the crowning glory
of a ride in the Savoie region of the French Alps
that is as peaceful as it is challenging.

There's something wonderful about France, and it's not just the landscape or the food or the people. It's also the language. Where else would you find a road as charmingly named as Les Lacets de Montvernier? Les Lacets, which translates as 'shoelaces' or 'sharp bends', refers to the stretch of tarmac that drapes and squiggles its way from the village of Pontamafrey-Montpascal via 18 hairpins up to the village of Montvernier.

Villages and tiny towns are a feature of this ride in the Savoie region of France. Saint-Jean-de-Maurienne, Fontcourverte-la-Toussuire and Modane have a combined population of less than 13,000, yet they gained significant investment and exposure from

hosting three stages in the 2015 Tour de France. That investment brought local infrastructure up to the race's exacting standards, while leaving the roads blissfully quiet afterwards. This route incorporates the very best and most famous in these parts, and from Les Lacets will take in the Col du Chaussy, the Col du Glandon and the Col de la Croix de Fer.

The ride starts in the narrow, sleepy streets of Saint- Jean-de-Maurienne, from which you head north out of town along the back roads adjacent to the A43. A few kilometres further on, past a landscape that mixes industrial furniture, idyllic houses and babbling rivers, you reach the foot of Les Lacets. At 3.4km (just over 2 miles) long and nudging 8%, it isn't an easy climb, but fresh legs and the waterfall carving its path through the rock alongside you make for a relaxed, gloriously peaceful ascent as the towns below quietly fade away as you near the top.

You'll soon pass through Montvernier and onto the Col du Chaussy proper, and as you press on, the road is swallowed up by trees as the vista of the Maurienne Valley below disappears in a sea of vibrant green. Eventually the treeline breaks, and if the views at Les Lacets were good, the views from near the top of the Col du Chaussy are spectacular. Far in the distance, patches of snow melt into slate-grey rock and lush green flora. Flanking either side of the valley below, they create a V-shaped gap on the horizon through which Saint-Jean-de-Maurienne is just visible in the haze. Prior to 2015, the Col du Chaussy hadn't made it into the Tour, >>

La Chambre

Col du Chaussy

Les Lacets

Saint-Jean-de-Maurienne

Col du Glandon

Le Mollard

Col de la Croix de Fer

La Saussaz

Villages and tiny towns are a feature of this ride in the Savoie region of France

>> largely because of a lack of connecting roads, making it an up-and-back journey. But thanks to works completed in 2012, it became ripe for the Tour's picking, and it's a truly spectacular addition.

Like an oasis in the desert, a café at the col's summit creeps into view and is the perfect place to stop for caffeine before the descent. It was a long drag uphill so you'd figure it would be a rip-roaring descent on the way back, and the Col du Chaussy doesn't disappoint.

Where the hairpins on Les Lacets were tight and compact, the Chaussy's are long and smooth, making it an exhilarating descent that you can take at high speed when conditions are good.

Once off the back of the col, you follow the D99 towards La Chambre, then take the D927 southwest towards Saint-Étienne-de-Cuines and on to the foot of the Col du Glandon. The first 10km (6 miles) of this climb are relatively straightforward ('relative' in the sense that the rest of it is even more difficult).

If you really enjoy climbing, the Glandon is for you, because it's the Col that keeps on rising ever upwards with false flats giving way to vicious spikes and all thoughts of single-digit gradients vanishing into the valley. Eventually we reach what you would assume is the top – and indeed it is – of the Glandon. But there are still a few hundred metres of road to go before you reach the real pinnacle in these parts, the Col de la Croix de Fer.

You descend for a moment before hastily punching your way to the top, where after all that climbing you will be grateful to see the Croix de Fer – the infamous iron cross on its concrete plinth that gives the col its name – set against the gnarled mountainous terrain. And from here there's a twisting path over which the road drops from nearly 2,000m (6,562ft) to a little over 400m (1,312ft). The road surface isn't quite so good on this stretch, especially if it rains, yet what discomfort there was on the climb up will be totally consumed by the thrilling excitement of this journey down.

From Saint-Sorlin-d'Arves you head east towards La Saussaz, then north to Le Mollard and the D110. This will deliver you back to Saint-Jean-de-Maurienne, where the tiny populations means that, unless you've brought your own army of admirers along with you, there will be precisely no one waiting about to greet you like a Tour-conquering hero. But that doesn't mean you can't feel like a hero.

Northern Europe

NORWAY
Atlantic Ocean Road

Norway's Atlantic Ocean Road is rated as one of the world's most spectacular routes to drive by car. It's even better by bike.

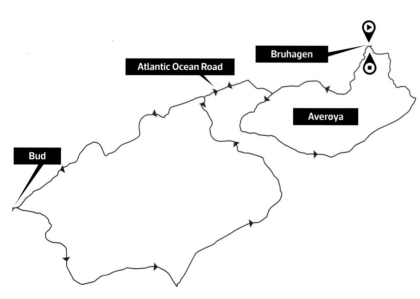

Bruhagen

Atlantic Ocean Road

Averøya

Bud

Cyclists are perfectly used to riding in wind and rain. We tend to have an extra coffee and put on some arm-warmers. In Norway, however, the concept of bad weather is slightly different. This is home to Thor, the thunder god, who has a penchant for letting rip with the kind of conditions normally seen only in Hollywood blockbusters about the dangers of global warming.

But it's worth catching a break in the weather, because the region – which is 311km (193 miles) north of Bergen – is a unique place to cycle. What it lacks in elevation it makes up for in a maze of inlets and islands and jagged, windswept coastline.

Distance: 150km *(93 miles) (approx)*
Elevation: 1,320m *(4,331ft)*

Then there's the miracle of modern engineering that is the Atlantic Ocean Road. In just 8km (5 miles) it packs in eight bridges and a plethora of viaducts and causeways, so that a series of tiny Norwegian islands is connected by a thin ribbon of tarmac that twists and rolls its way through the harsh coastal landscape. Completed in 1989, the string of bridges is so dramatic that it frequently plays a starring role in television commercials for cars, and the *Guardian* newspaper ranked it top of its list of 'world's best road trips'.

The road links the Norwegian mainland to the island of Averøya, next to which sits another island that's home to Kristiansund, a town of around 23,000

people. This ride begins (probably via a car from Kristiansund, which is where the airport is and makes for the perfect base) in the village of Bruhagen. You will take the 64 road towards the Atlantic Ocean Road, followed by a coastline-hugging meander, before cutting inland to complete a second pass of the Atlantic Ocean Road and a loop of the Averøya island, to finish back at Bruhagen.

You're likely to be hit with a full-frontal headwind, which means there's no chance of an easy roll-out to gently warm the legs as you head deeper into a wilderness of exposed rolling roads that slice their   >>

>> way through the barren, rock-strewn landscape. The road surface is good, but as the first glimpses of the ocean come into view it's hard to stay focused on the tarmac for wanting to gaze towards the endless horizon.

It's less than 16km (10 miles) to Kårvåg, the gateway village that guards the entrance to the eastern tip of the Atlantic Ocean Road. You're likely to be buffeted by even more wind as you ride through Kuholmen and over Little Lauvøysund Bridge to the isle of Lille Lauvøy. Then it's across the tiny islands of Eldhusøya and Lyngholmen. The road was hit by no less than 12 hurricanes during its construction from 1983 to 1989, so be thankful if all you have to face is a stiff breeze.

You're reduced to little more than a crawl as you climb the 8% gradient up the spine of the serpent-like, 260m- (853ft-) long Storseisundbrua cantilever bridge. The structure arcs out of the ocean as if to hurdle the municipal border between Averøy and Eide that runs beneath it. At the summit it's possible to see a distant silhouette of the mountains further inland.

Past Hulvågen, through Skarvøya and Strømsholmen – narrow islands, barely wide enough in places to contain the road – you rejoin the mainland after the final 119m- (390ft-) long Vevangstraumen Bridge.

Hug the coast along the narrow 242 road past the offshore rocky islets to join the 663 to Farstad, then hook a sharp right onto the 235 towards Hustad. Here, the headwind is likely to be even worse. Eventually you arrive at the beautiful fishing hamlet of Bud (pronounced B'you-ed). It's strange to imagine that a village so small, and with so much charm, was the largest trading port between Bergen and Trondheim in the 16th–17th centuries. It's the ideal lunch stop, especially if you like fish.

Once back on the road, you join the 664 south towards Tornes along the Julsundet Strait at the mouth of the Frænfjorden. The pace is brisk as you

A maze of inlets and islands and jagged, windswept coastline

then head east and the road becomes a blur of grass-roofed fishing huts and undulating bends through which you can top 70km/h (43mph). Then join the 64 to Eide and drop your pace to fully absorb the delights of the Kvernesfjord en route around the Averøya island and back to the finish at Bruhagen.

The snake of road, arching and twisting across its rocky stepping stones, is laid out before you as you reach the Atlantic Ocean Road. Stamp on the pedals when you hit the first bridge and chase your lengthening shadows across the legendary 8-km (5-mile) stretch. If you have a bike computer, the screen will be completely blue, except for a thin vertical line up the middle. There's nothing else to obstruct the view. It's just road and sea.

Distance: **185km** *(115 miles)*
Elevation: **2,980m** *(9,777ft)*

ENGLAND
Yorkshire Dales

Inspired by the Tour de France's Grand Départ, this Yorkshire ride takes in the best bits of 2014's opening stage with a few extra treats that the pros didn't get to see.

The profile details for the opening stage of the 2014 Tour de France included one reassuring word: flat. You might therefore think that a ride through the Yorkshire countryside – a region that since the Grand Départ came to visit has established its own pro race (the Tour de Yorkshire) and hosted the World Championships in 2019 – is going to be fast and friendly. Trust us, the one thing this ride is not is flat.

There's no denying that the Tour's 2014 visit to Britain was a special event. Yes, the race had made the trip over the Channel before, but it had never ventured further than the capital. This time the Tour plunged deep into the English heartland to showcase British roads to the world, and they made a big impression.

This ride takes a 'highlight reel' approach to the region, focusing on the glorious Dales. It starts just south of Skipton town centre, where the Tour route passed when some 50km (31 miles) into Stage 1 in 2014, and you amble into action along Grassington Road. Once you hit the small town of the same name, after about 15km (9 miles), the road narrows and you take in some striking views. The first of these comes as you pass Kilnsey Crag overhanging the road. A limestone cliff that stands 60m (197ft) tall, it's a reminder that you're in a land of rich natural beauty. It's also a land of lumps, because you'll soon have covered 30km (19 miles) with scarcely a single flat section longer than 100m (109yd).

Kidstones is the first true climb of the day, and it wastes no time in setting the tone. Snaking up alongside a stream, it shifts from a reasonable 5% to a punishing 15% in just a few hundred metres. It then teases you by easing off slightly, only to reveal an even steeper section ahead. From the summit, however, a long and open descent lies ahead of you.

After that plunge downhill, you roll back into the undulations that characterize the route, albeit ones with a few more dips than spikes. It's a winding and technical route that keeps you entertained even   >>

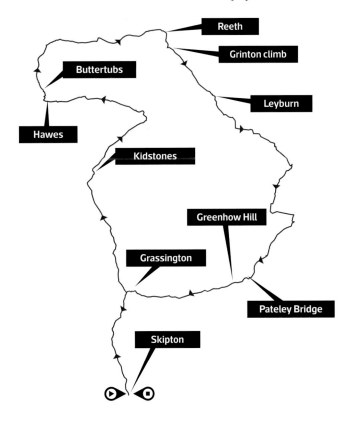

Reeth

Grinton climb

Buttertubs

Leyburn

Hawes

Kidstones

Greenhow Hill

Grassington

Pateley Bridge

Skipton

>> during the lulls between the hills. You make your way through Aysgarth and skirt along the River Ure, rising once again as you approach Hawes, where a right turn separates you from the next challenge.

Buttertubs is a formidable climb – don't let the cute name fool you – which rises to a height of 555m (1,821ft) over 4.5km (2¾ miles). A signpost warns of 17% gradients, but Buttertubs is actually a pleasant ascent. The meat of the incline averages around 6% and is broken up by easier sections that offer moments of respite. Take the early stages at a steady pace and you'll have enough left in the legs to attack the punishing 20% gradient that comes 100m (109yd) before the summit.

The valleys and rolling hills sprawl out beneath the shadows of the Pennines and, with the road snaking ahead in full sight, the 20-km (12½-mile) descent begs to be taken at speed. The small town of Reeth is a good place to eat, and once back on the bike you quickly run into your first obstacle of the return journey: the Grinton climb. It spikes up to an aggressive 15% in places until the crest of the hill heralds another 10km (6 miles) of descent, before a series of fast undulations takes you into Masham.

Turn off the main road past the market and you'll plunge into the deepest Dales. As you ride along the single-track and at times gravel-laden road, you will leave behind you telegraph pylons, cars and all signs of modernity as you pass stone walls, battered picket fences and grazing horses. Stay on that road until you see a left turn for Grewelthorpe, and at the T-junction turn right and then left after 100m (109yd). Take a hard right when you reach Kirkby Malzeard, and at the next junction turn right to Pateley Bridge, a charming village that appears to have been built at the bottom of a deep pit. This is undoubtedly the most challenging part of the ride, with the gravelly descent narrow, blind on every corner and so very steep at 20–25%.

The only way out is upwards, and as you head out west towards Skipton a 20% sign warns you of trouble ahead. This is the famous Greenhow Hill, which gains 290m (951ft) of elevation in barely 4km (2½ miles) and spikes well above 20% in parts. Once over the top, you skirt along fields of heather and can build momentum as the road undulates and descends. Grassington soon pops into view, and from here all that's left is to complete the loop in Skipton. However you choose to classify this route – flat, lumpy or bonkers – you will see why the world of cycling fell in love with the Dales of Yorkshire.

IRELAND
Ring of Kerry

The Ring of Kerry is a spectacular lap of one of Ireland's
most westerly peninsulas, and it's a whole
land of adventure in itself.

There are landscapes that are impressive due to their vast scale and dramatic geology, and then there are those that just seem to have an air of magic about them. This ride takes you to one such other-worldly place, the Gap of Dunloe, wedged into Ireland's highest mountain range, with a narrow lace of asphalt threaded through an enchanted landscape of lush green grass and pitch-black boulders. For this alone it's worth the visit, but you're to be treated to so much more besides.

This route is based loosely on the Ring of Kerry, a popular tourist pilgrimage around the coast of the Iveragh Peninsula, but has been adapted slightly to start in Killarney. From there it cuts southwest through the middle of the peninsula to take in two passes before rejoining the Ring, and then diverting inland once more for a dramatic crescendo at the Gap.

Cycle out of Killarney past the striking St Mary's Cathedral, an impressive structure for a settlement of 14,000 inhabitants, on the main N72. After 6km (3¾ miles) on the flat, you turn left onto Gap Road, which is where your adventure begins. The road is named after the Gap of Dunloe, but for now you ride past the left turning that would take you there, and continue into rural Kerry. The road is narrow and quiet, and to your left looms the Macgillycuddy's Reeks mountain range.

You soon find yourself on the first gentle climb to Lough Acoose. The landscape is rocky on both sides, with sheep nibbling on the uneven grassy hillsides and a patchwork of bracken, yellow gorse and heather decorating the verges. You're reminded that you're in the Emerald Isle by a hundred subtle shades of green, and at the summit the tranquil waters of Lough Acoose reflect the hills beyond it.

After the first climb comes a refreshing descent through trees that opens out onto plains, where your next climb is revealed. The Ballaghisheen Pass is 5km (3 miles) long, starting with a kilometre (⅔ mile) at 6% followed by a gentle 3km (just under 2 miles) of around 3% that allows you to admire the green plains falling to your left and more rocky hills to your right. Then it kicks up to 11% for the last kilometre (⅔ mile), with a steep   >>

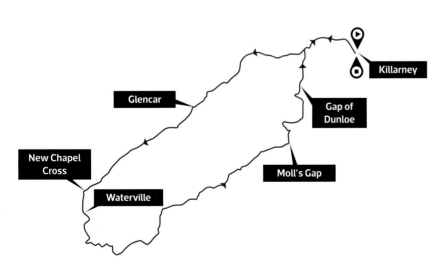

Glencar

New Chapel Cross

Waterville

Killarney

Gap of Dunloe

Moll's Gap

Distance: 153km *(95 miles)*
Elevation: 2,029m *(6,657ft)*

A narrow lace
of asphalt
threaded through
an enchanted
landscape

>> right-hand hairpin delivering you to the summit. The rapid descent that follows feels like a mirror image of the climb, being steep at the top and easing off as the height drops away. Back on flat road, you now cover 15km (9 miles) to the junction with the N70 and turn left towards Waterville.

The seafront here is an ideal place to stop for lunch before the third climb of the day, which begins as soon as you leave town. You're on the Ring of Kerry proper

now, and a dramatic ascent that traverses a huge green and rocky bank while offering a glorious unfolding view of Ballinskelligs Bay. At the top of the climb it's worth pulling into the lay-by to take in the panoramic scenery while coach tourists browse a handful of stalls.

The descent from here is a string of gentle corners that demands your full attention but no braking. As the road flattens, you flash past the popular beaches near Castlecove. Then the road starts to climb gently

once again as you head inland to Sneem, a small town named after the river that flows under its bridges to the nearby estuary.

Here you leave the Ring and head inland once more, the road climbing for 10km (6 miles) towards Moll's Gap. Then, after a narrow and technical descent, the climb to the Gap of Dunloe is arduous, but the reward is spectacular. As you ascend through the final corners, a huge plateau of rock that appears before you on the left, and the equally impressive Purple Mountain on the right, form a V-shape ahead of you. Over the summit the road snakes like a narrow ribbon through a beautiful green wilderness. You need to concentrate to keep fatigue at bay because these technical roads could punish the weary. Thankfully, there's hardly any traffic at all, and this is no road for coaches. There's also no rush, because the scenery is incredible.

You cross a series of perfect arched stone bridges, the prettiest of which is known as the 'wishing bridge', before emerging into what looks like a perfect bowling lawn nestled between the mountains. A fairy-tale stream meanders through it and huge black rock boulders are wedged into its surface. It is unquestionably magical, and will lift your spirits as the light fades in proportion to your energy.

Continue the descent over the sometimes rough and gravelly roads to the right turn that will lead you back onto the N72 to Killarney. Here, St Mary's Cathedral will rise to greet you after a truly almighty day on the bike.

ENGLAND
Lake District

The views are spectacular in this part of Britain, so get ready to pay in sweat for the pleasure of seeing them.

I t's all too easy to treat Britain's climbs with disdain, especially if you've conquered Alpine peaks soaring above 2,000m (6,562ft). But there's a part of England that will make you realize how short-sighted you've been as you wipe the sweat from your eyes. A day riding in the Lake District is as tough as a day cycling anywhere that road tyres dare to roll.

The region is probably best known among cyclists for the Fred Whitton Challenge, commonly thought to be the hardest sportive on British soil. In the space of 180km (112 miles) the route clocks up an impressive 3,900m (12,795ft) of vertical gain, which is a profile comparable to the biggest players on the European sportive scene. The reason such elevation can be reached in an area somewhat lacking in Alpine peaks comes down to what >>

Cockermouth

Braithwaite

Keswick

Whinlatter Pass

Honister Pass

Kirkstone Pass

Ambleside

Distance: 140km *(87 miles)*
Elevation: 2,875m *(9,432ft)*

SCOTLAND

Scottish Borders

On this ride you'll head north to Peebles to experience its quiet roads, stunning views and rugged climbs.

Distance: 144km (*89 miles*)
Elevation: 1,790m (*5,873ft*)

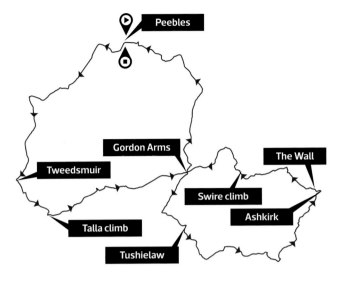

The people of the Scottish Borders are, on the whole, a friendly bunch. They're aware that they are the first Scots that English travellers meet on their way north, so the Borderers try to make a good impression on behalf of the whole country. This is possibly why the local bike shop will suggest you follow the loop of this route in an anticlockwise direction. Although it means you are heading into the wind in the early stages, you'll have the wind at your back when you hit the bigger ascents, notably the notorious Talla climb. There are some testing gradients in these parts, and you'll need all the help you can get.

This route therefore starts in the town of Peebles and heads west on the A72. Traffic is pretty minimal around here, but within a few kilometres you swing left over an old stone bridge across the River Tweed and away from the main road.

The land around the Borders is more rugged and sparse than the chocolate-box countryside of the Yorkshire Dales or the Lake District, but it's lush, green and rolling compared with the craggy mountains of the Highlands. The Borders hills are gently curved and soft with vegetation, but there's still a sense of remoteness that makes it perfect cycling territory.

You cruise along smooth, empty tarmac alongside the Talla Reservoir, which keeps the taps of Edinburgh running. The surrounding hills drop steeply into the water, and while your journey up until now has been relatively flat, the view up ahead suggests that soon your leisurely ride is going to be halted when the road runs out of level ground to cling to. Sure enough, around the bend at the end of the reservoir you're greeted by warning signs saying '20%'.

The Talla climb attracts cyclists from across Scotland, so approach with caution and settle into a steady rhythm as the road quickly ramps up to its maximum gradient. At the top you can catch your breath, drink in the views and salivate at the prospect of the long, sinuous descent that stretches ahead of you, winding through the valley towards St Mary's Loch.

Once you've blasted down the hill, the gradient levels out past Megget Reservoir before dropping away again to the junction at St Mary's Loch. A few kilometres of main road brings you to the Gordon Arms, which marks the crossroads for the route. You'll return here later, but this time you take a right and head towards Tushielaw.

Now back on bare roads, the landscape opens up as you climb up between rough fields separated by ➤➤

>> low dry stone walls and patches of heather. After about 5km (3 miles) of gentle ascent, the fields give way to a dense forest of pines, and the road swings left to reveal a fast descent. A right–left shimmy at the Tushielaw Inn brings you into more rolling countryside that undulates and twists through low hills and past streams.

Through the tiny village of Woll you hit a 4-km (2½-mile) climb known as 'The Wall', which is actually more of a long drag with the occasional kick up to 12%. Eventually the climb tilts down into a valley and across the ancient stone bridge that's the gateway to Ettrickbridge. About 15 seconds later you come out the other side of the village and find yourself back among the fields and woodland of the Borders landscape.

A right turn approximately 500m (⅓ mile) further on brings you to the foot of the toughest climb of the day: the Swire (aka Witchy Knowe). On paper this road doesn't instil fear – 2.5km (1½ miles) at an average 7% – but by now you've got 110km (68 miles) in the legs. You can only hope they're restored by the magnificence of the views over swollen hills blanketed by a patchwork of every shade of green. Then you rattle over the cattle grid at the summit to enjoy the fast drop to the valley of Yarrow Water, where you rejoin the A708 west back to the Gordon Arms.

This time you take the Peebles road and start the northward journey back to base, but there's still one more ascent to negotiate. Paddock Slack is a shallow haul of around 5km (3 miles) that would register fairly low on the pain scale when you're fresh but, 125km (78 miles) in, it's far more testing.

With 15km (9 miles) to go, you've seen off the last of the climbs, but the final stretch is lumpy enough to send tired legs into the red. There are still a few kilometres of woodland to cut through before the grey stone houses of Peebles appear. If the weather gods have been kind, you can enjoy a well-deserved ice cream on the river.

The Borders hills are gently curved and soft with vegetation

SCOTLAND
Scottish Highlands

Jutting into the North Atlantic Ocean like a giant thistle, the remote peninsula of Ardnamurchan offers a wild, rugged ride through the Scottish Highlands.

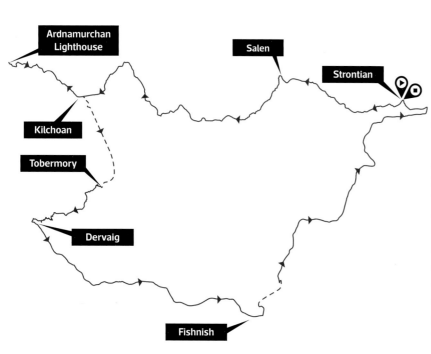

Ardnamurchan Lighthouse

Salen

Strontian

Kilchoan

Tobermory

Dervaig

Fishnish

Don't let Scotland's reputation for wet weather put you off this glorious cycle ride. The plentiful rain in these parts feeds the lochs, and the roads that weave around them in the Scottish Highlands make this an exhilarating place in which to ride your bike.

This route starts in Strontian, a small village 38km (24 miles) from Fort William (but twice that distance by road), and heads west on the A681 to Salen. It's worth fortifying yourself before you set out with a traditional breakfast of porridge oats, shortbread and copious amounts of tea because this is going to be a long day in the saddle.

Distance: 154km *(96 miles)*
Elevation: 1,299m *(4,262ft)*

You ride on the very edge of the northern side of Loch Sunart, which isn't a very fitting name given that this region is officially classified as a rainforest. A bit later on, you'll be riding around the rim of an old volcano, too. This really is a unique British ride.

From Salen you turn left onto the B8007, and the narrow single track hugs the shore towards Ardnamurchan Point, the most westerly spot on the British mainland. This part of the ride feels as if you are on a rollercoaster as the road constantly crests small headlands and swoops into bays in a serpent-like pattern along the lochside.

The road takes a turn inland for a short stretch, away from Loch Sunart for the first time, and the landscape changes to a more rugged, open moorland. It can look bleak in mist and rain, but if you catch some sun it's truly beautiful, and in the distance you can glimpse the isles of Eigg and Rùm.

There's also significantly more climbing now, especially from the village of Kilchoan as you tackle the last few kilometres to the Ardnamurchan lighthouse, with a final ramp up to its base. When you arrive there, the lighthouse stands proudly before you, unpainted in its natural granite. It first shone out to warn mariners of the treacherous, rock-strewn >>

>> headland in 1849. The lighthouse gives warning to this day, though it's been automated since 1988.

The ride to the lighthouse has taken you away from the loop, so you now need to backtrack to Kilchoan, but rest assured it's worth the detour. You can't hang around for too long under the giant red foghorn, however, because you've got a boat to catch. The route takes you over to Tobermory on the Isle of Mull, so plan ahead to get your timings right because the ferries from Kilchoan run only every couple of hours. The ride back to Kilchoan is only around 10km (6 miles) and predominantly downhill, so you'll soon be sitting on the lochside watching the ferry edge towards you.

Once you've made the crossing and your wheels are back on terra firma, lunch is just a few pedal strokes away up a steep little climb amid the row of brightly coloured houses for which Tobermory is famous. Then you begin the next part of your journey, to the village of Dervaig, which means heading inland up a fairly tough climb for about 5km (3 miles) before a rewarding descent down the other side through a series of switchbacks to Dervaig.

This is among the most picturesque parts of the ride, and at Dervaig you turn left onto the road south through the middle of Mull. Once again, ferry timetables will be on your mind because you've got to get back over to the mainland to complete the loop. The road opens out into a stunning valley, and the gradient lends itself to holding good speed as you carve between the hills, past bubbling streams and patches of tall pine trees.

When you head back towards the coast, you'll see signs for the A484, but don't expect some heaving highway because the main road on Mull is still predominantly single-track. You'll pass the wrecks of boats stuck in the muddy expanses left by the low tide,

Don't let Scotland's reputation for wet weather put you off this cycle ride

and you can up the tempo slightly ahead of the next ferry departure from Fishnish to the mainland.

Boarding your second ferry of the day and bidding farewell to Mull means that you've broken the back of the loop. There's only about 40km (25 miles) still to go, although you're faced with a long climb straight out of the ferry terminal at Lochaline. It begins as a gradual drag up a valley of open moorland on the single-track A884 before the terrain steepens for the last few kilometres to the ridge.

As you make the transition from climbing to descending, you're safe in the knowledge that you're now on the home stretch. Loch Sunart comes back into view for the first time in what will seem like a long while, and the fast descent back to Strontian is a perfect way to end the ride.

ENGLAND

Dartmoor

It seems in the UK that the more beautiful the place,
the tougher the ride. And you can test that theory to
its limit on the wild expanses of Dartmoor.

Dartmoor is one of those rare places in the south of England (southwest, to be exact) where, a mere 40km (25 miles) from the coast, the terrain changes from seaside towns to smooth, undulating tarmac that would make the Alps slap Devon on the back and ask to buy it a drink. The roads that traverse these parts are in superb condition, and when you set off, you may be met with Dartmoor's rich fog, which clings to the peaks and wallows in its troughs, the way fog does high up in the mountains.

This route starts in the village of North Bovey and heads north towards Moretonhampstead. Straight out of the blocks, you're climbing already, alongside dense woodland until the treeline breaks and the road flattens. That's just a warm-up, however, because

just outside Moretonhampstead you spear onto Cross Street and descend an almighty hill until you get to the bottom, at which point you turn around and climb back up the 20% incline. Fortunately it's only 500m (1/3 mile), and once you're back on the main road you'll be fully warmed up.

Turn left at the top for Bovey Tracey and here you will round a turn that brings you onto the B3387 towards Haytor. It's an average gradient of 6% that extends for 5km (3 miles). Along the way it takes in views of Haytor Rock, a giant granite outcrop that punctures Dartmoor's rolling hills.

Apparently a handrail and steps were built up the outcrop in the 19th century to help tourists climb it, something that was met with disdain by one punter who declared that this merely enabled the 'enervated and pinguedinous [fat and greasy] scions of humanity of this wonderful 19th century to gain the summit'. The rail has since rusted and only worn steps remain, but at 4km (2½ miles) up the adjacent road, you may well be wishing someone had thought to install a rail here, too.

By the time you reach the top you'll be in need of a breather, which comes in the form of a cooling descent towards Ponsworthy. As you skirt through the tiny hamlet, you catch sight of your next challenge, a 1.5-km (1-mile) slog that is steepest near the bottom, at 17%, then settles into a slightly more civilized 9%. As you peak, the landscape opens up once more and Dartmoor sprawls out around you, sliced in   >>

Moretonhampstead
North Bovey
Bovey Tracey
Two Bridges
Widecombe-in-the-Moor
Pork Hill
Princetown

Distance: **98km** *(61 miles)*
Elevation: **2,059m** *(6,755ft)*

Dartmoor sprawls out around you, sliced in half by a perfect cycling freeway

>> half by a perfect cycling freeway that stretches well over the horizon. The going's a little bit more forgiving now as you roll steadily through the landscape that Steven Spielberg referred to as having 'an abundance of natural beauty' during the filming of *War Horse*.

Just before the halfway mark, you reach Princetown, which is a logical place to stop and recharge the batteries. Once you're suitably rejuvenated, it's back on the bike to round the edge of the national park and

begin the climb of Pork Hill, but not before we rocket down one gloriously long descent through Yelverton. Don't get distracted, and keep a look out for Dartmoor Ponies on the road.

Depending on how you want to look at it, Pork Hill into Merrivale hillside is either a very, very long climb or two very long climbs, stitched in the middle by a tantalizing flat and a short descent that will leave you wondering if you're at the top. Beginning a few clicks east of Tavistock, it goes through Merrivale towards

Rundlestone at an average of just over 4%. No problem, you might well think but, at 7km (4⅓ miles) with more than 1,000m (3,281ft) already climbed, it hurts. It's also pretty straight, which means the incline is always looking back at you, staring you down like an angry man in a bar.

The second half of the climb hosts the annual Tavistock Wheelers' hill climb, a bruising event run by the local cycling club of the same name. Your legs may well be starting to feel leaden by the time you reach the top, so you'll be grateful for the whippy descent towards Postbridge and an undulating northeasterly path that takes you back towards your starting point.

You're now virtually home and dry, with a mere 8km (5 miles) to go. The route plan makes this bit look easy compared with the rest of the day, but that's without factoring in the 2,000m (6,562ft) climbing and the 90km (56 miles) travelled. And while it's an exhilarating rush through corner after corner, your legs will thank you when you finally hit the high hedgerows that signal you're back at North Bovey.

By now your muscles will be hinting that a two- to-one carb-protein mix might be a good idea, but, equally, your heart might be calling for a beer. There's no reason why you can't have both as you reflect on one of the most beautiful rides the UK has to offer.

Distance: 98km *(61 miles)*
Elevation: 1,583m *(5,194ft)*

BRITISH ISLES
Isle of Man

The Isle of Man has mythical status among cyclists. It's home to Cav, Kennaugh and many other pro cyclists who have honed their craft on some of the toughest roads in the British Isles.

The Isle of Man doesn't mess about. It's an epic place to ride a bike, with sections so steep you'll feel as if your back wheel is lifting off the ground on the way down. The roads are tight and narrow, twisting like a luge run through acutely angled, deeply cambered corners, up, down and pretty much all around. And that's before you even consider the weather, and the brutal winds that batter you on the coastal roads.

It's little wonder that this small island has produced a number of professionals. Eight Manx cyclists took part in the 2019 British Championships, while Peter Kennaugh, retired pro Jonny Bellis and, most notably of all, Mark Cavendish are all Manxmen. One ride here and you'll understand why the setting for the insanely dangerous TT motorcycle races makes cyclists so tough, too.

The route starts in the island's capital, Douglas, which is the logical place to stay given that this is where the ferry from Liverpool arrives. In fact, the ride starts at the Isle of Man TT race headquarters on Governor's Road, from where you drop down to the seafront and head south out of town to Fort Anne Road, along the coast to Marine Drive. Don't panic if you wake to be confronted by wind and rain. This is common, and a peculiarity of the island is that it usually brightens up by mid-morning. Usually.

Three hours on a bike here are like four on the mainland, according to locals. Young Manx riders have gone to England to train with British Cycling, returned home with training plans and then ripped them up, exhausted by the fact that they were having to ride so much harder here in the Isle of Man. Don't be fooled into thinking that this route's relatively short distance will make for an easy day on the bike.

Less than five minutes out of town you're straight up the first climb to Douglas Head, a steep and punchy ascent that takes you high above the Irish Sea on Marine Drive, a car-free stretch of road that is cut into the cliff. It's twisting and technical and there's no respite. You're descending, then out of the saddle as the road climbs before descending again, constantly shifting position, and on and off the >>

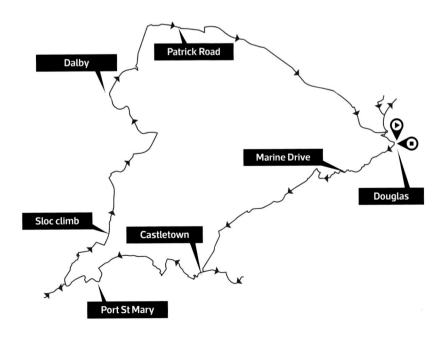

Patrick Road

Dalby

Marine Drive

Douglas

Sloc climb

Castletown

Port St Mary

>> brakes as the road twists and turns. Clearly, they don't do flat, or straight, on the Isle of Man.

The route takes you to Castletown, past the airport and over a causeway onto St Michael's Isle. The road becomes a track and you double back to Castletown and along the southern reach of the island towards Port St Mary. It's here that things get serious as you tackle two 6% hills in quick succession before you see the Calf of Man, a tiny, rocky outcrop jutting into the sea. The landscape is remote, craggy and hard, with further outcrops called the Anvil Rock and the Chasms being constantly blasted with waves. The scenery also has a cartoon-like quality, with every feature and colour exaggerated as if someone has turned up the contrast level to maximum. There's no time to admire the scenery, though, as you tackle another sharp descent.

Next you spin through Port Erin before heading out towards the Sloc on the west of the island, pressing on into a roaring wind up a 3-km (2-mile) climb that boasts several 10% sections. The Sloc itself is an imposing, gorse-covered crag through which the road rises straight up, with a kink to the right roughly at the halfway point.

Crest the first part of the climb and there's a short chance to recover on a small plateau before the gradient rises again, and hopefully the wind will help to push you up the final pitches. The descent is an adrenaline-fuelled blast as you whizz past Glen Rushen Plantation towards Dalby. You're inland now, and the landscape is heavy with pine forests and feels far calmer than the element-battered coast.

Finally you pick up the southern end of the TT course and chase back to Douglas. The terrain is still hilly, but the road surface is beautifully smooth. Pass through Crosby and you'll realize you've been riding in the big ring for more than two whole minutes – the first time that has happened today – as you head back into Douglas. The route may only have been just shy of 100km (62 miles), but your legs will certainly be letting you know you've done it.

You'll also understand why such a small island has honed such a tenacious winner as Mark Cavendish. The roads, with their constant angles, cambers and gradients, and the harshness of the ever-changing conditions, mean that all of the Manx tarmac really does feel tougher than 'normal' roads. Simply making forward progress can be a challenge as the island fights back with everything it has.

ENGLAND

North York Moors

The North York Moors may be less well trodden than England's other national parks, but the riding on offer is as challenging as it comes.

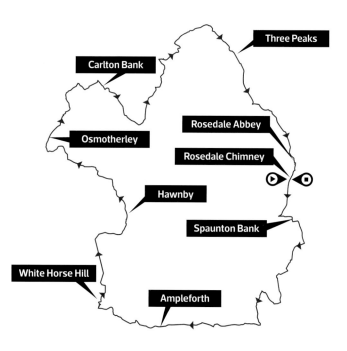

Three Peaks

Carlton Bank

Rosedale Abbey

Osmotherley

Rosedale Chimney

Hawnby

Spaunton Bank

White Horse Hill

Ampleforth

If you need convincing about the North York Moors' cycling credentials, try starting a ride with a leg-shattering slog up the steepest road in Britain. There's not even a hint of a warm-up: it's clip in, turn left out of the car park, 30% gradient. The Rosedale Chimney, as the near-vertical stretch of tarmac is called, is a challenge to be relished by any cyclist.

A sign reads, 'Rosedale Chimney Bank. Max gradient 1:3. Engage low gear,' but the Chimney is actually steeper than the 1-in-3 signs say it is. The good news, however, is that this ride starts at the White Horse Farm Inn, which is located

Distance: 130km *(81 miles)*
Elevation: 2,233m *(7,326ft)*

a quarter of the way up the climb. A gentle left takes you towards the first of many cattle grids of the day, before a short straight offers a postcard panorama of the North York Moors. Then it's into the Chimney's two severely steep hairpins, the second of which exits into what a bike computer will tell you is a momentary 56% gradient. It's lucky, really, that you're only three minutes into the ride.

The gradient eases to 20% towards the top, where you're welcomed by a slight descent that allows you to gather your breath. The empty, single-track road bisects exposed moorland full of purple heather, quite possibly a defining image of the ride.

After a few kilometres you sweep through a lazy left–right over a small bridge, and undulating countryside leads to the second bump of the day, the picturesque Spaunton Bank. After a few kilometres more, you're into the sleepy and isolated village of Appleton-le-Moors, where sheep nibble on the grass banks between the road and sandstone houses. It feels like something from another age.

From here you can enjoy 20km (12½ miles) of easy rolling farmland on the southeastern edge of the Moors. This is the only properly flat section of the day, so treat it as a belated warm-up. After a short stretch on the B1257 you turn off towards Ampleforth >>

>> and past the imposing abbey and school. The road zigzags up through Wass before the immense ruins of Byland Abbey loom up on the left, and then you enter the North York Moors National Park once more. Take an easy-to-miss right turn onto White Horse Hill and get ready for the next challenge.

The climb itself is steep and rewarding, and much more memorable than the famous White Horse figure cut into the hillside that gives the climb its name. High up on the Moors now, the remaining 80km (50 miles) of the route has a profile that looks like the blade of a saw. A fast 4-km (2½-mile) descent takes you across the River Rye and into Hawnby, which serves up a short, sharp, 25% mid-village climb.

With the River Rye on your left, you're into a non-stop series of picturesque climbs and descents across the paths of the tributaries to the Rye, which have cut themselves deep into the landscape over millennia. A 20% sign indicates a fast and dangerous descent past farm entrances and sheep fields. Steep banks on either side deposit mud and gravel into the road as it plunges down into Osmotherley, an ideal lunch spot.

The first hill on the post-lunch horizon is Carlton Bank, which has an elevation gain of 200m (656ft) over about 2km (1¼ miles) and features at least three severe kicks. The next tooth of the saw is Clay Bank, a steady, laborious climb on the B1257, the day's only significant stretch of main road. Then comes another gravelly, woody descent towards the final challenge of the ride. A cattle grid marks your re-entry to the Moors proper and you approach what's unofficially known as the Three Peaks, a series of challenging climbs culminating in the longest of the day. With 110km (68 miles) in the legs, you'll be out of the saddle for these, and partway through there's an exciting narrow descent, a sharp turn through a ford and an immediate kick up into a scenic climb that makes for the most exhilarating section of the ride.

Sheep nibble on the grass between the road and sandstone houses

The final climb is a 4.5-km (2¾-mile) drag with a couple of 20% sections that will squeeze the last drops of power from your legs. If the signature view of an Alpine ride is a ribbon of hairpins weaving into oblivion, the Moors are typified by long, single-lane paths stretching unwaveringly to the horizon. There's something deeply satisfying about a road's honest, arrow-straight trajectory, but it also allows no room for comforting delusions that the end of the climb might be just around the next corner.

The last 5km (3 miles) is a high-speed descent back into Rosedale Abbey, before the short climb up the nursery slopes of the Chimney to the White Horse Farm Inn once again. While it made for the toughest possible start, there are many worse places to finish.

WALES

Snowdonia

The hills of Snowdonia are better known as a magnet for hikers, but they offer riding of the highest quality and scenery to match.

Distance: 138km *(86 miles)*
Elevation: 2,329m *(7,641ft)*

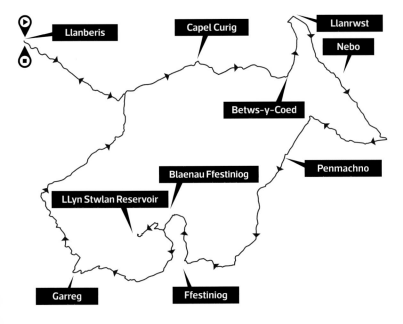

Llanberis
Capel Curig
Llanrwst
Nebo
Betws-y-Coed
Penmachno
Blaenau Ffestiniog
LLyn Stwlan Reservoir
Garreg
Ffestiniog

As legend has it, there was once a famous duel fought out in the mountains of Snowdonia between King Arthur and a giant named Rhitta Gawr, a colossus of such fearsome strength that he wore a cape made from the beards of kings he had vanquished. King Arthur, however, refused to give up his beard and 'clove him in twain' atop Snowdon.

Snowdonia doesn't have quite such a rich history of cycling as it does of mythical battles, which is baffling when you consider the undulating, quiet and often savagely steep roads here. On paper it seems too good to be true, even if you do have to be wary of the occasional angry giant.

This route draws a near-perfect picture of a dog, like a Strava Art image produced on a GPS computer, but the quality of the ride has not been sacrificed for the sake of art. Starting from Llanberis, you ride southeast on the A4086 along the banks of Llyn Peris (*llyn* means 'lake') at a decent pace as the valley up ahead begins to reveal an enticing climb that snakes up to a summit of 350m (1,148ft). The incline sticks to a consistent 3–5% as you ascend in the shadow of Snowdon, until the road spikes up to more than 10% before the top and then gives way to a thrilling descent.

As you skirt down the side of the hill, you're rewarded with a view of Snowdonia's plunging landscape, with the scenic Llyn Gwynant glinting between two hillsides to your left. At Capel Curig turn right onto the A5 to the pretty village of Betws-y-Coed, and turn left as the route begins to extend into the most northerly part of Snowdonia. You snake up into more woody and hilly terrain approaching the Nebo Road climb, which takes you from sea level straight up to 314m (1,030ft). Hedgerows and trees shelter the climb, but the forestry breaks occasionally for long enough for you to peek at the valley that extends to your right. The road tilts up to 10% again near the summit, and then some winding, technical descents separate you from the biggest road of the day, the A5. Despite the name, it's surprisingly quiet.

Turning south towards Penmachno, you make your way to the second sting in today's route, a 300-m (984-ft) climb on the B4407. A cattle grid marks the beginning of the ascent, which has taken you into a narrow track that winds through dense forestry on its way to a spike of 20% near the top. Over the summit the track begins to resemble a road again as you turn right to Ffestiniog and sweep through the historic mining town of Blaenau Ffestiniog, which has a   >>

>> rugged and scenic charm. From here, you turn left at a big roundabout (signposted Porthmadog) onto the A496 until a right turn to Tanygrisiau takes you to what is undoubtedly the highlight of the ride.

The climb up to the Llyn Stwlan Reservoir, which begins at a turning past the Tanygrisiau Reservoir and just before a small bridge, could well be the UK's best-kept cycling secret. It's a 3-km (2-mile) gravel road that averages 10%, with spikes of 20%, en route to the impressive dam that forms the eastern edge of the reservoir.

The mere existence of this tightly winding, steep and thin road is a little baffling in this part of the world. The Stwlan climb boasts tight switchbacks – which look more like the Stelvio Pass in the Alps than anything you might expect in the back roads of Wales – and a view that will leave you breathless.

The start is marked by an industrial gate, as the road is actually a route for maintenance workers to reach the Stwlan Dam. Set amid craggy rocks, the ascent gives way to an open view of the valley below, with the arches of the dam ahead of you, luring you forwards. It's steep enough that you quickly find yourself looking over most of Snowdonia, and when you reach the reservoir it possesses a huge natural presence that complements the mountainside.

The road to the dam is a dead end, so double back down the incline, taking care on the occasionally loose surface. At the bottom of the climb, turn right and continue to the junction with the A487, where you turn right towards Porthmadog, then right on the B4410 towards Rhyd. At Garreg, turn right on the A4085 towards Beddgelert, then right on the A498 to Capel Curig. Along the way, you pass two majestic lakes (Llyn Mair and Llyn Gwynant) and a river, Afon Glaslyn, before tackling the big ascent to Pen-y-Pass. The road winds around from the south through a grinding climb that joins up with the first descent of the day, taking you back to 350m (1,148ft) altitude before you arrive back in Llanberis, probably feeling dog tired.

This route draws a near-perfect picture of a dog

NORTHERN IRELAND
Emerald Coast

Enjoy the best bits of what the professionals experienced
– and a whole lot more – when Northern Ireland hosted
the start of the Giro d'Italia in 2014.

It can have an invigorating effect on a region when a Grand Tour comes to town, and that was the case for Northern Ireland when the Giro d'Italia took to the roads around Belfast for the opening stages of the 2014 edition. Keen cyclists visit the region or see the roads and the backdrops on television and want to explore them for themselves.

This point-to-point route starts in Portrush on the northern coast, which is where riders in Stage 2 of the 2014 Giro d'Italia turned east before tracking back down the coast to Belfast, where this ride will finish in 196km (122 miles). By the time they got to Portrush, they had completed around 80km (50 miles). However, you're going to omit that first slog in favour of swinging inland before rejoining the Giro's route.

Follow the A2 east past the Bushmills Distillery towards the Giant's Causeway and it will become clear that riding here is rather more exotic than in other UK cycling destinations. Not exotic in the sense of palm trees and coconuts, but in the sense of a road with sheer drops to the sea to one side and sweeping panoramas to the other. The only thing to remind you that you're in the UK is the occasional British-style road sign.

The sign for the turn-off to the Giant's Causeway will grab your attention in particular. While it's not on the route – at a high spring tide it's not implausible for the road to literally end in the sea – you can catch a bus down the steep road to where the Causeway begins. What greets you when you get there is, frankly, astonishing. Great rock columns of varying heights rise in eerie regimental conformity, each perfectly tessellating with the next to give the impression of a fossilized mountain city or some gargantuan arcane cathedral.

After the bus ride back up, you continue on your way before turning left onto the A2/ Whitepark Road. Soon you take a detour down towards Ballintoy Harbour, a tiny stone fishing port that looks like it would be far more at home in children's television than moonlighting as it has as a filming location in the TV series *Game of Thrones*. You're treated to a series of steep, tight switchbacks that do their best to expose any chinks in your cornering armour. And there's no bus back up this climb, so once you reach the bottom you'll be out of the saddle to grind your way back to the top. >>

Portrush

Cushendall

Carrickfergus

Whitehead

Belfast

Distance: 196km *(122 miles)*
Elevation: 2,400m *(7,874ft)*

Riding here is rather more exotic than in other UK cycling destinations

>> Instead of diving down the A2 towards Cushendall as the Giro did, you turn off at Ballyvoy and take the narrower and more exposed Torr Road. A glorious length of tarmac rises up and wends its way along the coastline, with just a 1m- (3ft-) wide verge and a few barriers to separate you from the crashing sea below. About 6km (4 miles) in, the gradient flips and you're suddenly hurtling down a series of turns that have a lot more in common with a spiral staircase than they have with a road.

The trick to riding rolling roads is to stay fast, which means laying down the power while trying to maintain cadence. To do this requires maximizing the speed of the downs and making well-timed shifts through the ups. With 22km (14km) of open road ahead, you have plenty of time to practise.

In Cushendall you turn up the A2/Loughareema Road and head north to Ballycastle. By this point you'll probably find yourself battling the wind, because in just 10km (6 miles) you've dropped from 350m (1,148ft) to a mere 8m (26ft) above sea level, and the shelter of the hills seems a distant memory.

From here it's an exposed, flat drag back along the coast down Glenshesk Road. Take a left down Coolkeeran Road, then head east down Altarichard Road and back to the coast, which will accompany you down to Whitehead and through Carrickfergus. To your left runs a beach that comprises nearly as much collapsed dry stone wall as it does pebbles, while to your right tower craggy cliffs as you make the final run towards the finish in Belfast.

There are no rolling hills or tranquil loughs here, and – with the exception of the capricious conditions of places such as the Alps or the Pyrenees – you're unlikely to have experienced such a dramatic shift in environment over a single ride. The Emerald Isle really is something of an untapped gem.

IRELAND
Connemara

A visit to the very outskirts of Europe reveals quiet lanes and stunning scenery in Connemara.

Distance: 118km *(73 miles)*
Elevation: 688m *(2,257ft)*

Teetering on the edge of the Atlantic Ocean on the western coast of Ireland is the unspoiled province of Connemara. It's a spot so tranquil, so secluded, that philosopher Ludwig Wittgenstein once called it 'the last pool of darkness in Europe' and escaped civilization here in pursuit of a higher level of thought. While electrification has shed a little more light on its charms, it remains a rare refuge from modern living, and a cycling haven.

Life in Connemara can be summarized in two words: quiet and slow. That definitely makes it ideal for cycling. This route starts in the small town of Clifden, from where you head north on the N59 and ride straight onto the gentle ascent of the Sky Road, a road that draws tourist attention from far and wide, balancing as it does over cliffs and the Atlantic Ocean. The waters glow with that turquoise blue you only see in travel advertisements, while on the other side of you are misty hillocks surrounded by hawthorn trees.

After tracking along the coast, the road eventually snakes inland. You churn uphill, passing through tiny villages as the sea shrinks to the horizon, and then you turn back downhill where a technical descent leads you to an inlet with a flotilla of fishing boats. The road offers an animated, fast-paced roll through the coastal scenery despite its heavy, undulating surface.

You bid farewell to the Sky Road at a junction where you turn left to stay on the N59 for another 20km (12½ miles) of thin, winding roads over the northerly coast. In fact, these narrow coastal lanes aren't dissimilar to the Sky Road but are peppered with a few more signs of civilization. You skirt quickly through the picture-postcard fishing village of Cleggan before arriving at a harbour marked by a stone beach. From here you make your way up into wild, rugged hills. The approach to the first of today's loughs (small lakes), Ballynakill, is steep enough to persuade you out of the saddle. In these inner regions of Connemara, the orange and red complexion of the land and the dilapidated stone walls make it feel as if you're in a time capsule.

Depart from Ballynakill Lough and head southeast to Garraunbaun Lough, and once again rejoin the N59. Despite its being the largest highway in the area, there's very little difference, save for a modest white line in the middle of the road. You ride through a >>

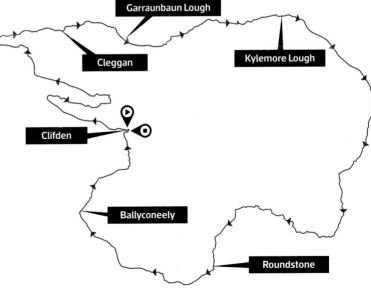

>> corridor of trees, where the sun flickers through the branches and makes patterns on the road, before arriving at one of the region's most notable attractions, Kylemore Abbey. This Benedictine monastery, which was formerly Kylemore Castle, is one of the scenic highlights of the trip. They also serve up a good lunch.

It's not until you are back on the road that you get a complete view of the vast neogothic building. Seen across Kylemore Lough, against a hilly backdrop, it couldn't be better suited to the landscape. As you roll down the N59, the scenery remains similar but the terrain changes significantly. Having enjoyed the coastal undulations of the Sky Road, you're now on endless straight and windswept roads. Once past Kylemore Lough, you turn right onto the R344 and continue until reaching the N59 once again. Turn right and then take the second left, turning onto the R340 to head south, and work your way over a 10% spike that persists for 1km (²/₃ mile) or so.

When you are over the top, you can enjoy a downhill whirl to the sea, where you join the R342 coast road. This becomes the R341 as it winds in and out of the rocky cliff faces. It's here that the riding becomes the most technical and challenging, the tight bends chasing one another over the undulations.

By now the evening light should be shining over the Atlantic as you approach the village of Roundstone and the road rises up along the cliff edge. The houses along this stretch are distinct, each a different pastel colour, but you soon leave them behind and, with the road mainly downhill from here, hug the coast past tiny thatched cottages and local inns through Ballyconneely.

The final run, back to Clifden, is rougher than usual, with potholes and patches of gravel scattered liberally over the lumpy surface. But in a funny way it feels less like a hazard and something more akin to the challenge of Paris–Roubaix (see page 82), where you simply have to dip your head and churn through while your muscles work to preserve momentum. And with the work that your muscles have put in today, the final sweeping downhill road into Clifden, with its wide-angle view over the ocean, will come as a blessed relief.

Connemara is a rare refuge from modern living

WALES
Pembrokeshire

Part monumental ride, part pub crawl,
the western coast of Wales offers everything
a rider could ever want.

It looks like an ordinary castle but, rumour has it, the one you pass when you are around 50km (31 miles) into this ride around the coastline along St Brides Bay was owned, until relatively recently, by Led Zeppelin. And while this far-flung corner of the Welsh countryside seems an unlikely retreat for the famously overindulgent rock band, maybe everyone needs a little solitude sometimes.

Pembrokeshire is a serene place, and the coastline – all 420km (261 miles) of it – is renowned for its rugged cliffs, beautiful beaches and charming harbours dotted with pastel-coloured houses and rich greenery. In this coastal region, the roads have a delightful habit of swooping down into picture-postcard bays, but just as quickly as they draw you in, they make you turn and climb steeply back out. They are far better explored by bicycle than they are by car.

You start this route by heading south on the A40 from Wolf's Castle, before turning right at Ford soon after. Continue towards Hayscastle Cross, then turn right on the B4330 and left towards Roch. All the while you're treated to panoramic views of the coastline, until you cross the A487 and turn right on Welsh Road to Newgale, where you ride right next to the pebble beach. From here you rejoin the A487 to the tiny fishing village of Solva, where fishing boats and dinghies bob up and down on crystal-clear water like a scene from a travel brochure.

Around 30km (19 miles) into the ride, you pass through St Davids, which has the distinction of being Britain's smallest city, thanks to the stunning cathedral that sits at its centre. Here you embark on an extra-short loop that takes you down steep twists and turns to the pretty little inlet of Porthclais before re-entering St Davids from the other side to get a different perspective of the cathedral.

Leaving St Davids again, this time heading northwest, you hug the coastline once more through the villages of Berea and Trefin in the direction of Abercastle. Continue to track the coast northwards as the tarmac rolls like a sine wave towards Fishguard. There might not be any 2,000-m (6,562-ft) cols around these parts – in fact, Pembrokeshire is often described as being flat – but the continual ups and downs have a fatiguing effect on the legs. >>

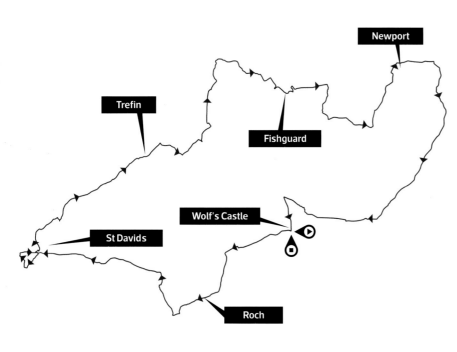

Distance: 132km *(82 miles)*
Elevation: 2,558m *(8,392ft)*

You pass through St Davids, which has the distinction of being Britain's smallest city

>> Eventually the road starts to descend, and as you round a left-hand hairpin on Goodwick Hill, still well above Fishguard, you're treated to a superb view of its harbour. The road here is practically straight and, with a good line of sight, you can pick up speed rapidly as the landscape turns into a blur.

At the bottom you skirt around the town and head out of Fishguard, leaving behind the coastline that's been such a feature of the ride and going inland on

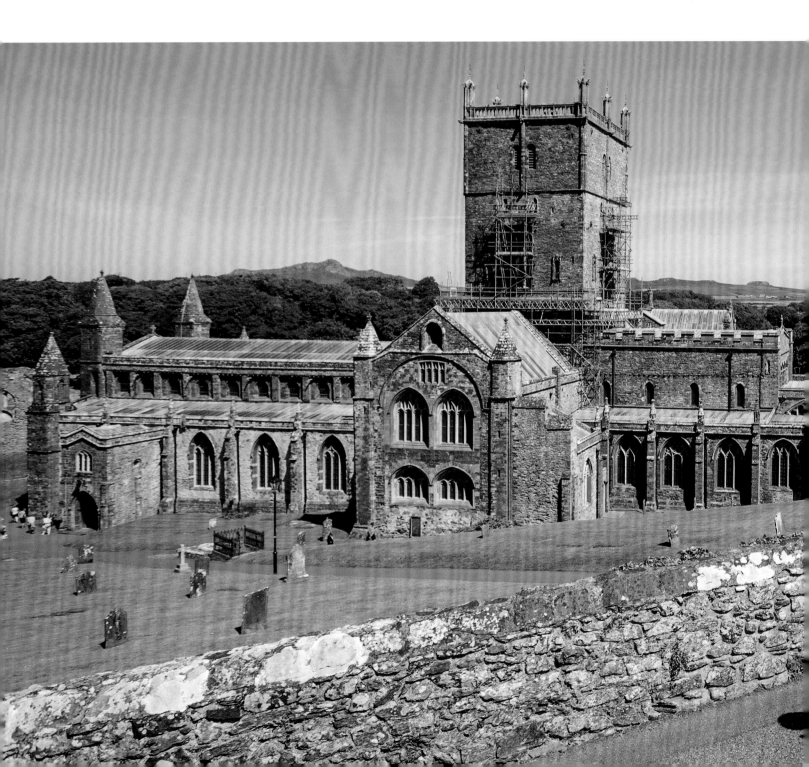

the A487 into the heart of the Pembrokeshire Coast National Park. Don't forget to look back down over Fishguard because it is even prettier from your new vantage point on this side.

Turning right off the A487 towards Llanychaer, you are now well within the national park boundary. Here the roads are once again narrow, high-hedged and winding. The steep switchback descent takes you to a left turn off the B4313 and through Clyn Wood and Pontfaen all the way to the valley floor en route

to Cilrhedyn Bridge. The road narrows even more, but the riding is superb and the backdrop lush. You now find yourself on the valley floor, which means you ride straight into a climb, and it's a brute. The road points upwards steeply, leading to several switchbacks that do little to alleviate the gradient. After a while, the slope relents but continues to gain altitude steadily for some distance. Eventually you crest the summit and begin the exhilarating descent that will take you all the way back down to the coast and the A487, to the small town of Newport, the most northerly point of the loop.

You're about 100km (62 miles) into the ride, so now you start the ascent that bisects the national park and points you back towards the starting point. You're hemmed in by high hedgerows and trees for the lower reaches of the climb before being launched into wide-open moorland. The breeze is cooling but the downside is that you're left in no doubt about what lies ahead because the remainder of the long climb is visible all the way to the summit.

Cresting the high point of the ride at just over 400m (1,312ft), you're treated to a dizzying 360-degree view of the county. It's practically all downhill from here, and on a road that's straight and visible for long stretches. There's lots of scope for eye-watering speeds as you race down the B4329 beyond Tufton, before turning left onto the A40 back to Wolf's Castle. Who was it who said Pembrokeshire was flat?

ENGLAND

Western Cornwall

Skirting the dramatic cliffs of western Cornwall will take you on a ride of undulating moors, shady lanes and harbour towns where the cake stops come with lashings of clotted cream.

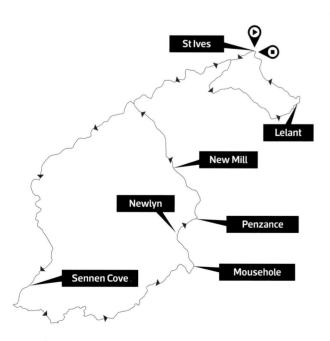

St Ives

Lelant

New Mill

Newlyn

Penzance

Sennen Cove

Mousehole

Some of Cornwall's dry stone walls are thousands of years old, but the hills are even older and some of them feel like walls, too, when you're riding up them.

This southernmost county of England has a reputation for being one of the sunniest places in the country, but it also deserves a reputation for being one of the best for cycling. Within 30 minutes of the start, you'll have ridden past rock tors, granite spires and high ridges, and gazed at distant cliffs that tumble into the sea. All the while you can see the route in the distance meandering away from you like a rollercoaster.

Distance: 87km *(54 miles)*
Elevation: 1,307m *(4,288ft)*

This route hugs the coast from St Ives to Penzance and then circles back over the moors via a second loop to St Ives. The coast is wilder and more rugged than the lush, green tourist honeypots of Newquay, Padstow and Rock further northeast. Remote moorland dominates this part of the county, and on the coast the land appears to drop vertically into the sea. Take the B3306 southwest from St Ives to Land's End, which follows the rolling contours of the coast in a series of ebbs and flows that make it perfect cycling territory.

At West Penwith you'll find the Carn Galver tin mine, a relic of the area's industrial heyday. It's an impressive sight, where you can pause to check out the eerie shell of the old pump house and engine room. The road, flattening out a little beyond here, is smooth but is also decorated with cattle grids and, occasionally, cattle. Be patient with them.

Next you're on your way to St Just, mainland Britain's most westerly town, which lies in an official Area of Outstanding Natural Beauty. There's a nasty 21% surprise before you get there, but once you are up the hill and through town, passing Land's End Airport, the road flattens. To the west is Sennen Cove, a surfing beach and coastal village at the bottom of a very short, steep hill, but you avoid this and after around >>

>> 10km (6 miles) you take a left towards Treen. This is where you can stop for a little of whatever you fancy, so long as it's accompanied by clotted cream.

Back on the bike you enter a magical world of flowers and high hedges. The road from Land's End to Mousehole is a tunnel of towering foxgloves, pink campions and overarching trees. If the wind is up, the banks of flora will swirl in the breeze and surround you with flying petals. You're now on the route of the Land's End 100, a 161-km (100-mile) sportive that takes place in October and offers a generous serving of suffering alongside the scenery.

Turn off the B3315 towards Mousehole (pronounced 'mowzel'). The descent into town via Raginnis Hill is a seriously steep, 1.5-km (1-mile) single-track road. The reward for this treacherous 18% decline is a stunning view of the turquoise waters of Mousehole harbour and St Clement's Isle, a rocky outcrop a few hundred metres out to sea. Winding through a crisscross of narrow streets and past stone fishing cottages takes you to the harbour, where the road tilts inexorably upwards as you attack the hill out of the village.

Follow the Cliff Road to Newlyn, home to one of the UK's largest fishing fleets, and press on into Penzance, the biggest town in the area. This is also a good place to stop for calories, but don't overdo it because, while the climb out of Penzance up Gear Hill doesn't look too tough on paper, it will feel long and gruelling if you're weighed down by a big lunch.

After around 4km (2½ miles) you take a left to New Mill through the tranquil Trevaylor Woods, where beech, oak, sycamore and pine trees line the road. After around 2km (1¼ miles) the hedges recede to reveal spectacular moorland flecked with rashes of bright purple heather, and the flat road across the moor is a brilliant place to stretch your legs. The solitude lasts until you cruise down a hill to rejoin

This route hugs the coast from St Ives to Penzance

the B3306, and by this point on the ride you have only around 15km (9 miles) ahead of you to go. Unfortunately for your legs, that includes a challenge known as 'The Eagle Has Flown the Nest'.

This stretch peaks at around 14%, but with only a few kilometres to go you can empty the tank all the way up to the summit before enjoying a pleasant downhill ride to the B3311. This is followed by a sharp right around Towednack Hill. From here the moors rise sharply to the west, but you drop down into St Ives through Lelant and Carbis Bay. Refreshments are on offer in St Ives, of course, and after a ride like this you may well find you have room for just a *bit* more clotted cream.

The Rest of the World

Distance: 177km *(110 miles)*
Elevation: 3,419m *(11,217ft)*

MOROCCO
Atlas Mountains

There's more to Morocco than tagines and camels. Easy to reach and with perfect weather, the roads and mountains south of Marrakesh make for an epic cycling venue.

The joys of cycling in Morocco can perhaps be described best by what happens late on in this ride. You'll find yourself losing altitude faster than you can lose money in Vegas on the 40-km (25-mile) descent out of the mountains, which will be over your left shoulder, their white caps tinted pink and falling away from view. The mountains will also be treating you to the most amazing orange evening sky you've ever seen. Yet even after the sun has set you'll be warm, and you won't be able to stop yourself from thinking about friends at home commuting through rain and freezing temperatures in full winter gear. But that's not to say riding in Morocco is predictable.

This route starts in the town of Oumnass, which is southeast of Marrakesh and about a 20-minute drive from the city on the P2009. Once saddled up, you take this road south out of Oumnass to Aguergour before heading southeast on the P2024. This continues through the villages on the edge of the looming Atlas Mountains and the beautiful Kik Plateau for about 35km (22 miles) to a junction with the R203. Turn

right into the bustling market town of Asni, where you can stock up on food and water – and oranges, because the ones grown here will likely be sweeter than any you have tasted anywhere else.

Turn left out of Asni onto a rocky, twisting road, which, according to local printed maps, doesn't exist, but which does provide a much more scenic route than a lengthy dogleg east. You'll join the P2028 and continue to the junction with the P2030, where you turn right to climb up to Oukaimeden.

The best time to come here is in spring, around March, which is cooler and damper than in summer, yet you'll be surprised at just how luscious and green the landscape is. Morocco is far from being the parched desert you might have been expecting, given that it's only a stone's throw from the Sahara. But if the greenery comes as a surprise, your scheduled lunch stop is genuinely bizarre, because Oukaimeden is actually a ski resort. And, with about 3,000m (9,842ft) of climbing to do to get there, it's little wonder you can see snow on the mountains up ahead.　　>>

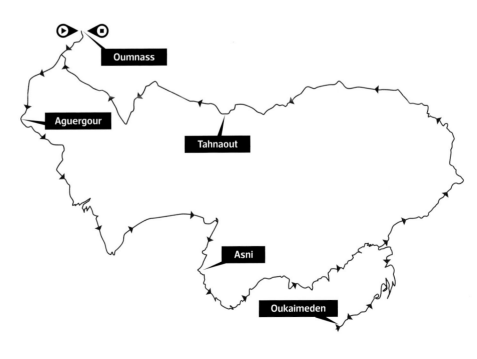

Oumnass

Aguergour

Tahnaout

Asni

Oukaimeden

>> The ascent is a brute in length at around 20km (12½ miles), but not so tough in gradient. It's never more than 7% and only infrequently reaches that. As you make your way up the winding route, you'll be looking forward to the descent, because you'll be coming back this way later on. The scenery gets more rugged and dramatic as you near the top, while at the summit it becomes downright strange. Here you will find yourself eating your lunch surrounded by people wearing salopettes and ski goggles.

You'll have been riding for more than four hours by this point, so it will come as a relief that the remainder of the ride is largely downhill, and the next 40km (25 miles) or so should whizz by in the blink of an eye. The curves are perfect for fast but safe descending, with sweeping apexes and good lines of sight, although a few sections of poor road surface should ensure you keep your wits about you.

By the time you reach the Ourika Valley floor after the 20-km (12½-mile) descent from the ski resort, the temperature will have risen sharply again and the chill of the mountain will be long gone. Turn right onto the P2028 again and follow it to the P2017 and P2010, which will bring you in a big loop round to Tahnaout and the last leg back to Oumnass. The stretch towards Tahnaout is likely the first vaguely busy stretch of road you'll have seen since the start. During the rush hour lorries will pass with dozens of people clinging to their sides. You'll also see plenty of mopeds, because in Morocco the humble moped appears to be the equivalent of a family saloon. They'll be loaded with adults, children, animals and more besides.

Even though our cycle route doesn't go through Marrakesh, it is only a 26-km (16-mile) drive by car or taxi from Oumnass. The city is an extravaganza of colour, noise and activity in its many souks and rabbit warren of tiny, twisting streets. More than two million tourists visit the city each year to revel in its richness and diversity. African in the geographic sense, Arab in culture, Islamic in religion and predominantly French-speaking, a visit to this city is a fantastic experience with or without a bike.

Morocco is a strange and magical place. If you're poring over an atlas for potential riding destinations and you can see beyond the Alps, the Dolomites, Mallorca and the rest, you won't be disappointed by a trip to Morocco.

Distance: 80km *(50 miles)*
Elevation: 2,578m *(8,458ft)*

UNITED STATES
Rocky Mountains

Boulder, Colorado, is home to America's best cyclists. And once your tyres hit the road, it's not difficult to see the reason why.

The dirt roads of Boulder, Colorado may feel strangely familiar, but this is probably the result of watching too many cowboy films. The town came into being in the middle of the Colorado Gold Rush of the mid-19th century, and little did the prospectors realize that their mountain tracks were creating a future utopia for endurance athletes. With its high altitude, jagged peaks and three hundred days of sunshine, it's no wonder that American pros Tyler Hamilton, Taylor Phinney and Andy Hampsten have called Boulder home.

Positioned as the city is, at the edge of the Rockies, all roads west of Boulder go straight up, and several of them gain over 1,000m (3,281ft) of height and stretch towards 3,000m (9,842ft) of altitude. One of the best-known climbs is Flagstaff Road, which rises for 8km (5 miles) at an average of more than 8%, and starts at a lung-punishing height of 1,750m (5,741ft). It's also the first climb on this route. Just 2km (1¼ miles) into it, you get your first taste of its demanding, 10% slopes. The road is surprisingly Alpine in nature, with tight hairpins and varied undulations, until you reach a section near the summit that locals dub 'the Wall'. A pair of hairpins begins the ramp, which spikes up to more than 20%. From there it's a 300-m (330-yd) stretch that lingers over 15%.

Once you've crested the summit, there's respite in the form of a steep but short descent on Colorado's flawless tarmac, but soon you have to rein in the speed as the surface turns to loose and patchy gravel. This is the rural treasure of the Rockies, with wooden picket fences and log cabins set into the hillside.

You turn right off Flagstaff Road and onto Gross Dam Road, which is where the real dirt begins. To call these roads gravel would be a little harsh, given that they're more like the chalky paths of Italy's Strade Bianche, the race held on white gravel in Tuscany. Once you have climbed the track you are rewarded with a stunning view of Gross Reservoir, which nestles in the mountain valley and mocks you with its inviting, clear blue water in which swimming is not allowed.

The descent has two stings in the tail. First, there are 'the breakers', a succession of tight bumps on   >>

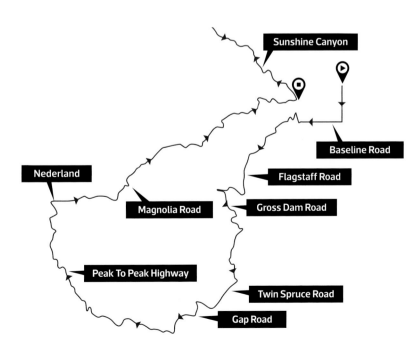

>> the road that feel akin to a white-knuckle ride over the cobbles of Roubaix (see page 82). Second, the descent then turns into a punishing climb, with gradients that hover around the 5–10% mark for 300m (984ft) of vertical ascent. It would be tough on tarmac, but on this surface you're reduced to near walking pace. To add to the challenge, the air is noticeably thinner at an altitude of nearly 2,500m (8,202ft).

Once you're over the summit, you descend to the blissful tarmac of Coal Creek Canyon, then climb Twin Spruce Road, to Gap Road. Muddy tracks on the tarmac suggest another dirt road isn't far away, and there's still 7km (4⅓ miles) to the summit. At just under 3,000m (9,842ft) it's the highest point of the day. There are rocky peaks on either side of the road and a panoramic view of the mountain ranges all around, but now it's time to retreat to the thicker air further down the mountain.

There's more dirt on the way down before you eventually emerge onto the tarmac of the Peak to Peak Highway. It has a fair amount of traffic but is so wide and carries such low speed limits that there's never a hint of intimidation from the passing lorries.

Rolling towards the town of Nederland, you turn right onto another dirt road, which then changes back to tarmac before a couple of smooth hairpins that arrive at a point just above Boulder Creek. Here you join a canyon road overshadowed by soaring cliff faces and tracking a fast-flowing stream.

Next up is Sunshine Canyon, which offers a mixture of tarmac and dirt, with the upper slopes winding up to 2,500m (8,202ft), making it the best part of a 900-m (2,953-ft) ascent over 14.5km (9 miles). The forests that line the road turn to open fields demarcated with split-rail log fences that seem to date from the 19th century.

From the summit you turn back to descend the precarious dirt-covered slopes, whose hairpins create an amazing panorama. When the road switches back to tarmac, you will feel like you've been turbo-boosted as your speed rockets up in an instant. The roads of Colorado – well paved, open and consistent in gradient – are perfect for descents. The scenery that's whizzing past as you gather speed changes from sparse pine to more lush greenery all the way back into Boulder.

There's a lot packed into this ride but it will still feel as if there's so much in Boulder that you haven't done. In every direction are roads that wind into the mountain wilderness. For any awed cyclist, this truly is an undiscovered frontier.

VIETNAM
Northern Vietnam

Sharing a border with China, northern Vietnam offers a host of incredible sights and a wealth of great riding.

Hanoi hits your senses like a tsunami. Stepping into the street is a bewildering experience thanks to the stifling air and a cacophony of shrill toots from the sea of mopeds that somehow manage to avoid either total gridlock or a mass pile-up. The idea of riding a bike in the middle of all this is frightening, but don't be put off. Everyone here has things to do, places to be, and the mopeds miraculously move out of the way once you're among them. No one has time to waste on crashing.

That's just as well, because Vietnam is without doubt an extraordinary place to ride a bike. This two-day ride actually starts via motorized transport (four wheels, not two) in Hà Giang, the capital of Hà Giang province some 270km (168 miles) north of Hanoi. Day one will take you from Hà Giang   >>

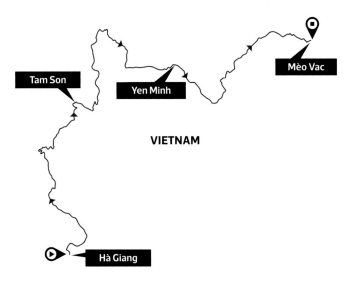

Distance: 153km *(95 miles)*
Elevation: 3,182m *(10,440ft)*

>> to Tam Son, where you will stay before setting off on your bike for Mèo Vac on day two. Both days will assault your senses – particularly those of sight and smell – in a completely different way to Hanoi, but one that's even more rewarding.

The first few pedal strokes in unknown territory are always exhilarating, but as you roll out on your first day, under the archway that marks Hà Giang's gate, the already sublime scene becomes ethereal. While the expanse behind you is flat, ahead lie huge mountains, unchanged for millennia. It feels like that scene in a movie when the road is quiet and the air heavy and syrupy sweet, before a tornado whips into town. From here you make a vertical ascent of nearly 1km (²/₃ mile) over the next 40km (25 miles) before you arrive in Tam Son, where you will have booked a hotel for the night. In fact, preparation is key all round, because if you get caught in a storm it could well be biblical. Hardy tyres are a good idea and lights are essential.

If the ascent to the summit was spectacular, down the other side the descent is something else entirely. Occasionally there are cat's eyes and reflective road markings, but in the main it's a hair-raising plunge into an unknown chasm of potholed switchbacks and sheer drops. Eventually you round a corner to see a dizzying array of neon lights strung up over an archway because, as in Hà Giang, two archways mark Tam Son's city limits, with houses, restaurants and hotels sandwiched between them. Now you can relax in your hotel before setting off again the following morning.

The contrast between the two days is striking. Whereas the ride to Tam Son was remote, on day two you'll be met by all manner of people, from weather-beaten old men herding water buffalo to elderly women bent double under mammoth sacks of rice. In fact, the only things looking like they're having a harder time than these diminutive yet powerful females are the mopeds whining painfully past

them. Apparently there are 37 million mopeds and motorcycles in Vietnam – and that's just the ones that are registered. In rural parts mopeds play the role of tractor and truck. You'll likely see livestock, mattresses and even washing machines being transported on these beleaguered 50cc workhorses.

From Tam Son you're heading for Mèo Vac, and the initial climb is shrouded in morning fog that turns the paddy fields and dirt tracks into large daubs of green and streaks of brown. But as you descend, then plateau and finally rise again, northern Vietnam begins to reveal her wiles.

In other countries a single mountain range would suffice, but here for each set of peaks there is another, even higher set behind, ascending in jagged grey strokes to the heavens. The air is sweet again with wild lavender and peach blossom. Dotted along the verges are rows and rows of beehives making honey, which you'll be able to sample when you happen upon one of the region's roadside pop-up restaurants.

Not even the food can compare with your lookout point, however. Stretched far into the distance are perfectly uniform terraces, cut into the hillsides to turn steep gradients into arable land, and below lies the dense vegetation of a valley all but untouched by human hand.

Next to you in the bark of a tree are some curious carvings made by farmers tapping the tree for sap, which they mix with petrol to form a glue to repair tyres. If you'd wondered what the locals did for puncture repair kits, now you know, but like so many things Vietnamese there isn't time for daydreaming. They just get on and do it. Much like you need to now.

Time is of the essence and there's no escaping the fact that there's still a lengthy descent to your end goal of Mèo Vac. Night-time riding in Vietnam is quite an experience, but one that's best enjoyed without sheer drops waiting to catch you out.

BHUTAN
Lower Himalayas

Nestled in the Himalayas, the Kingdom of Bhutan only recently opened its doors – and its high mountain passes – to Western tourists.

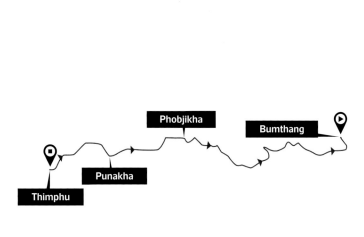

Why Bhutan? It's a question you'll be asked a lot if you plan to take your bike there. One glance at this Himalayan landscape, though, and the answer seems obvious. This is true mountain territory. The peaks feel like the prehistoric ancestors of the Alps in that they are bigger and steeper, hotter at the bottom, colder at the top, and blasted by Himalayan winds. It's truly epic terrain to tackle on your bicycle.

This route tracks across the main national highway (a one-track mountain lane), from Bumthang in the east of the country to the capital, Thimphu, in the west. You will be covering the

Distance: 268km *(167 miles)*
Elevation: 4,450m *(14,600ft)*

268-km (167-mile) distance over three days of riding, so you will need some form of support vehicle. It takes in three gigantic climbs in the Lower Himalayan Range: the Yutang La, Pele La and Dochu La. All three top 3,000m (9,842ft) of altitude, while only brief stretches of the route drop below 2,000m (6,562ft).

It's a complex place. Ancient temples set into the desolate mountainsides overlook fast-expanding neon cities. This ride to the capital is like an accelerated history of the nation, with much of the vast landscape differing very little from the mountain wilderness that greeted missionaries in the 17th century.

That blend of ancient tradition and modern world couldn't be more apparent as you climb the Yutang La, which peaks at 3,400m (11,155ft). The scene would have been little different 300 years ago, aside from the yak herders talking on their mobile phones today. The roads may lack modern-day quality, but they make up for it with breathtaking views. Every bit of the ascent is as technical as a crit circuit and as undulating as a Grand Tour queen stage.

As you tip over the summit, the scenery switches from lush and grassy to sparse and dry, and the descent is taxing, requiring you to scan the sketchy road surface ahead for cows or yaks. It's tough, but >>

>> also some of the most fun you'll have on a road bike. By the time you reach the base of the descent, the mountain valley still drops away for more than 1,000m (3,281ft) below you, and the next climb will take you upwards again for 2,000m (6,562ft) of elevation over 70km (43½ miles) to the peak.

Cut off from the rest of the world, Bhutan existed as a collection of small fiefdoms and warring regions until relatively recently. The Royal Family and religion are the two hinges of national identity there. Despite being Buddhist, the Bhutanese still have a strong belief in spirits of all kinds, and the roads are lined with altars, relics and shrines. Often their walls are covered with paintings to welcome good spirits and ward off evil ones.

Night will be falling as you near the summit of the Pele La, and the low light will illuminate to stunning effect the mist sitting in the valley below. A set of white flags marks the peak, and the first day is over. The logical place to stay is in a hotel in the nearby Phobjikha Valley, because tomorrow morning you'll return to the summit by car for the long descent to Wangdue Phodrang.

The downwards journey takes place on the Lateral Road, a route that was the consequence of Indian and Nepalese efforts to increase international stability, and which is still maintained by the Indian Border Road Organization. This side of the valley has the exotic landscape of a rainforest, but the road is so technical and undulating that you'll barely have time to appreciate it.

Back on smoother roads at the bottom, the ride to the bustling riverside town of Wangdue Phodrang is the most leisurely you will have experienced so far. Grab a spot of lunch and head to the ancient capital of Punakha for the evening, because tomorrow you'll take on the legendary climb of the Dochu La, which rises for 37.5km (23⅓ miles) at 5%.

This is truly epic terrain to tackle on your bicycle

Climbing the endless slopes on day three, you realize that travellers must have had to envisage a utopia on the other side of the peak to summon the determination to cross it. Yet it's stunning. With thick cedar trees and sheer cliff faces, it feels as if you're riding through the set of *Jurassic Park*, and the views across the Himalayan landscape are overwhelming when the trees clear.

It's more than two hours before you will catch a glimpse of the summit, and the heat falls away as you near it. When you finally reach the cluster of flags at the top, you roll to a halt at the base of a monument erected to honour 108 Bhutanese soldiers who died fighting Indian rebels in 2003.

From here you coast down to the capital of Thimphu (unless the wind is against you). But even with the savage winds and never-ending climbs, the beauty of the region keeps you moving, always desperate to see what lies over the next ridge.

ETHIOPIA

Northern Highlands

Thanks to pristine new roads, Ethiopia is now an exciting destination for cyclists.
Expect tough climbs, friendly people and views that go on for ever.

Distance: 130km *(81 miles)*
Elevation: 3,167m *(10,390ft)*

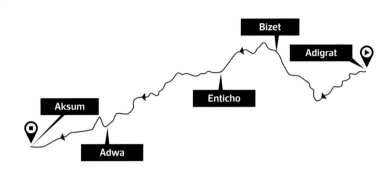

Anthropologists believe it was about two hundred thousand years ago that modern humans originated in Africa. After another hundred thousand years, they set out to colonize the rest of the world, by all accounts starting in the Horn of Africa, in what is now Ethiopia. By fifty thousand years ago, humans were in Europe. It then took another 49,800 years for mankind's greatest achievement – the bicycle – to be invented. Leap forward to the present day and cyclists are discovering why it's well worth a journey back to where it all began: Ethiopia.

True, the landlocked country in northeast Africa is still at the mercy of its climate, as demonstrated by the famine that hit it in 2016, but it's politically stable and is one of the fastest-growing economies in the world. China has invested heavily here in dams, railways and a road network, mainly in the Tigray Region in Ethiopia's northern highlands, the location for this ride. The roads have helped improve commerce and have reduced the impact of drought, but they've also had one unexpected effect – the region is now a wonderful place to ride a bike.

Loops are tricky here, so this is a point-to-point route that starts in the welcoming town of Adigrat and will finish in historic Aksum. Keeping a close eye on the tuk-tuks that buzz around the streets, you roll out of town heading west towards Adwa on Route 2, straight into the biggest climb of the day. You quickly leave urbanization behind and climb into a landscape of earthy brown terraces dotted with green shrubs and trees, the temperature rising quickly.

Soon the gradient creeps up, too, and the altitude makes itself known. This climb started at almost 2,500m (8,202ft) – the height of the biggest cols in the Alps – and you're now rising to over 3,000m (9,842ft), higher than almost any road in Europe. Up here it's not just the views that are breathtaking.

Once over the top you can take in a sight that's like no other you'll see on a bike. Stretching far into the distance are crags and canyons of soft brown rock, looking like the American Wild West but on a grander scale. Beneath a cloudless blue sky a complex network of valleys is fringed by sheer cliffs and bordered by dusty plains, while through it all runs a perfect ribbon of tarmac that descends in long, sinuous curves.

At around the 30-km (18½-mile) mark, the road suddenly drops away to the right, and a glance over the stone barrier reveals a sight to gladden the heart of any cyclist: a series of tight hairpins ressembling a coiled >>

>> spring, plunging into the valley below. Once you've dispatched those, it's a flat run to the town of Bizet, where you'd be well advised to refill your bidons.

From here the road becomes more rolling, with climbs of up to 10% followed by flowing descents. Although you're neither gaining nor losing altitude, the road is rarely flat, and the increasing heat ensures you'll be working hard. The payoff is that the scenery remains spectacular, with endless views over the parched plains. This is topped off at the 60-km (37-mile) mark, when a push over the crest of a hill reveals the Adwa Mountains. Sitting on the horizon like a giant collection of rock sculptures, the mountains resemble some lost prehistoric world, and in the distance you can see the road winding deep into their heart.

The perspective on the Adwa Mountains keeps changing as you ride, and the giant shapes grow and morph as you get closer. Eventually you're among them, and the road twists and turns as it picks a line through the maze of hills to the next town on the route, Enticho, which is the ideal place to stop for lunch.

Back on the road, there's a mercifully flat section before a 14-km (9-mile) uphill drag will have you puffing once more in the thin air. It's another 40km (25 miles) of magnificent, barren landscapes and towers of crumbling rock between Enticho and the next town, Adwa, and from here you're on the home stretch to your final destination of Aksum. In fact, you're now just 20km (12½ miles) away. Unfortunately, 10km (6 miles) of that is uphill, and you're already still at a high altitude. If you're lucky, you can shelter in the shade of a lorry as you climb, because most vehicles here will struggle up the incline as much as you do.

Eventually the road levels out and you're on the outskirts of Aksum. This was the seat of the ancient Axumite Empire, which stretches back more than two millennia. Today the town is a UNESCO World Heritage Site. It is also the site of Ethiopia's oldest Christian sanctuary, the Tsion Mariam church (dating from the fourth century but rebuilt several times since then), which claims to contain the Ark of the Covenant. Nothing about this place is ordinary.

It's not just the views that are breathtaking

UNITED STATES
Pikes Peak

Rising out of the Colorado plains is the mighty Pikes Peak,
a piece of American history, a motorsport paradise
and one of cycling's best-kept secrets.

It was 15 November 1806 when Lieutenant Zebulon Montgomery Pike first sighted what he called the 'Grand Peak', commenting that it was so high that 'no man could have climbed to its pinical [sic]'. When he initially spotted the mountain he was 193km (120 miles) away and, at first, thought it to be a distant blue cloud. As you approach Colorado Springs and see it looming up far away, you may well wonder how any road could go up such a desolate, gigantic mountainside. But go up it does.

Pikes Peak has a heritage that makes it distinct from the rest of Colorado's 53 'fourteeners', the name that was given to mountains surpassing 4,267m (14,000ft). The annual International Hill Climb, a world-renowned event on the motorsport calendar, has played an important part in that mythology. For cyclists, access to the climb was once restricted to a single organized race per year, but in 2013 the authorities opened the Pikes Peak Highway to cyclists all year round.

Starting from the small town of Manitou Springs, the road rises 2,361m (7,746ft) over 40km (25 miles), with only a false flat 800m (½ mile) long for relief roughly halfway up. The average gradient is 7%, and the summit sits at 4,302m (14,114ft) of altitude. It's the second-highest paved road in the US, only 4.5m (15ft) shorter than the highway that goes to the top of neighbouring Mount Evans. In terms of continuous ascent, though, Pikes Peak is the most testing climb in Colorado and one of the most challenging and incredible ascents on Earth.

There is only one way up, and the Pikes Peak Highway is the jewel of the region in riding terms. To get to it you travel along Manitou Avenue, the main road through the valley, on a 5% gradient, with jagged red rocks teetering overhead. The road skirts a gorge before passing through a tunnel to Route 24. While this six-lane highway is busy, motorists are generally respectful.

After 5km (3 miles) you reach Cascade, where you turn onto a quieter lane that leads you to the Pikes Peak Highway. A 15% ramp welcomes you, and at an altitude of around 2,500m (8,202ft) – close to the height of the Col du Galibier in the French Alps – you will notice how thin the air is already.

You have to pay a toll, and then you enter the realms of a national park. Pine trees >>

Highway Tollgate

Crystal Creek Reservoir

Cascade

Glen Cove

Manitou Springs

Pikes Peak summit

Distance: 116km *(72 miles)*
Elevation: 3,265m *(10,712ft)*

The land ahead is home to wild bears, rattlesnakes and mountain lions

>> and junipers surround you, with thick, mountainous forest smothering the land ahead, which is home to wild bears, rattlesnakes and mountain lions.

Riding a bike with a compact chainset is a smart move here, so you can find a rhythm at a low intensity. You have several hours of uninterrupted ascent ahead, and altitude sickness can be brutal if you overdo things.

After 4km (2½ miles) on the highway, you scale the edge of a mountainside where pine trees fall away from the steep banks of the road, which rises

to 15–20% for a few hundred metres. The route curves around the cliff edge ahead, where the gradient eases and the thick forest briefly separates to give a glimpse of the summit. Crystal Creek Reservoir offers the only respite from the climb – an 800-m (875-yd) descent followed by a brief freewheel over the flat road that runs along the eastern end of the reservoir.

At around 3,000m (9,842ft) the scenery changes dramatically. The luscious greens of the foothills give way to an arid, sandy landscape and the trees grow thin, tall and often deformed – they're known as flag trees. Then there's the 'alpine zone', which starts at Glen Cove at 3,500m (11,483ft), where no trees dare to grow. It's a barren and bare terrain, with few animals, low temperatures and sparse air. A desert, basically.

Pikes Peak isn't just long. Parts of its 40km (25 miles) are relentlessly steep as well, rising to 10% for long distances. You might not enjoy the usual anticipation of nearing a summit, which actually gives the climb a unique feel. You just steadily work your way up.

By now it's as if you've set foot on Martian soil, and there's a clear vista of the mountain ahead of you. The contrast between the snowcapped Rockies in the distance and the vast, flat Colorado plains is like an altitude-induced hallucination.

The temperature drops, snow is lining the road and the wind picks up. The road becomes a maze of switchbacks, overlapping and decorating the exposed mountainside, and the summit escapes from view as you ascend the upper ridges. Eventually you see the final climb and it's a mountain in itself, with three peaks to negotiate before you round the final corner. When you reach the summit you can expect to feel a deep elation – no doubt amplified by oxygen deprivation – that you may well never feel again, not even on what is almost certainly going to be the greatest descent you will ever experience in your life as you retrace the route back down to Manitou Springs.

CHINA
Hong Kong

With its blend of dense cityscape and quiet countryside, Hong Kong makes a unique place to ride a bike.

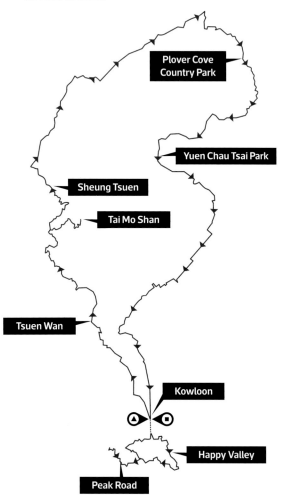

Plover Cove Country Park

Yuen Chau Tsai Park

Sheung Tsuen

Tai Mo Shan

Tsuen Wan

Kowloon

Happy Valley

Peak Road

Hong Kong is chaotic, a region that seems to somehow outpace itself, with every corner of the city alive with activity. Like much of China, it has seen a recent explosion in road cycling, and although it may not seem like an obvious riding venue, there are plenty of escape routes for local cyclists. Many head out to Lantau Island, where the western coast is still rich with wildlife and forests. Some circle Hong Kong Island and finish up overlooking the city on Victoria Peak. Then there's the New Territories, once the rural backwater to the bustling city of Kowloon on the mainland.

Distance: 123km *(76 miles)*
Elevation: 2,759m *(9,052ft)*

This ride will take in Hong Kong's two most iconic climbs: the first, Tai Mo Shan (the highest peak in Hong Kong), and the second, Victoria Peak (the highest on Hong Kong Island). The route starts in Kowloon, heading from Lo Wai in the north of the city along the coast towards Tsuen Wan and the first climb. It only takes a couple of turns off the main road before you find yourself on a wide, empty road with a leg-warming 10% incline. Immediately the buzz of the city fades away as you head into the rural expanse of the New Territories.

The temperature creeps up despite cloud covering the sky above you. Hong Kong often has this strange mixture of sunshine and cloud – it's known as 'the haze', and it's one of the reasons the government is encouraging cycling. The summit you're heading for is an observatory at 950m (3,117ft), 13km (8 miles) away, which will take you above the smog of the city. The first 6km (3¾ miles) ticks by with only the occasional steep ramp to negotiate, and as you climb higher you begin to understand why Tai Mo Shan is so popular. The views over the city are incredible.

Eventually the straight road becomes a series of tightly packed hairpins as you near the summit, where you're greeted by a high-security fence and warnings not to take photos. It's an excellent

>> climb but there isn't much reason to linger, so now you can dive into the descent, which is narrow but open enough that you can see what's up ahead and carve through the corners. Before you know it, you're back at the main road and turning right to head north, deeper into the New Territories. You pass through Sheung Tsuen village to Plover Cove Country Park, then follow the forest road back towards Kowloon, taking the picturesque coastal bike path from Yuen Chau Tsai Park.

For the second climb, you head to the main island for the iconic Victoria Peak. To catch the ferry to Central Hong Kong, you could set off at 6am, as most locals do, and cycle to the ferry port. However, the traffic is chaotic and often hostile, so it's probably worth hopping in a cab that can accommodate a bicycle to get to the ferry port.

Rising to an elevation of 552m (1,811ft), Victoria Peak is a surprisingly serious climb for the middle of a metropolis. It's 6.7km (4 miles) to the summit, and the longest constant stretch of ascent runs for 5.4km (3⅓ miles) at 5%. On paper it's a breeze compared with Tai Mo Shan, but this climb offers a very different experience of Hong Kong, including a fair amount of traffic to contend with.

Sitting right in the middle of the island, Victoria Peak was for many years almost uninhabited and inaccessible. Its height spared it from development during the early period of British colonialism, and it became a sanctuary in the centre of the metropolis. It was here that British governors built their summer homes, and to this day houses on Peak Road are some of the most expensive in the world.

The ascent starts in Happy Valley, heading up Stubbs Road and through a forest that offers glimpses of the urban sprawl through gaps in the trees. Stubbs Road turns into Peak Road at an enormous hairpin, where the traffic calms a little before you're treated to a breathtaking view across high-rise buildings clustered

Immediately the buzz of the city fades away

on the mountainside. In the distance is a view of the South China Sea being pierced by peaks covered in dense forest.

Near the top, you turn onto the narrower Mount Austin Road, which leads to the Peak Gardens at the summit. The surroundings are so leafy that it feels as if you're in the grounds of an English stately home, and as you reach the gardens you're greeted by pavilions and manicured lawns. This is where the summer residence of various governors of Hong Kong once stood. Known as Mountain Lodge, for 80 years it was famous among the British.

If you time your descent right, towards dusk, you'll see the sun move below the cloudy haze and a warm light flood the side of the Peak, bouncing off the glass and metal of its flanks. As you drift down the slopes, you know there is nowhere else on Earth that can offer a view like this from a bike.

ISRAEL

Negev Desert & Dead Sea

In Israel's southern heart lies the Negev Desert, a spectacular world of scorching sands where the roads dive down below sea level.

Vast. For a short word, it describes so much. Vast are the oceans, the mountains and the skies. And here, so incredibly vast is the Negev Desert. It seems impossible that there is anything more to Israel than the golden sands of the desert.

There is, of course. To the north lie mountains, to the west are beaches famed for surf and white sands, and to the east a sprawling patchwork of vineyards, groves and lush farmland. But you're here for the desert, and for two rides, the second of which offers a unique experience on a bike. About halfway down the western side of the Dead Sea, Highway 90 dips nearly 400m (1,312ft) below sea level. Cyclists often seek the highest roads that can be found, but what might it be like to cycle the lowest? In this case the lowest road on Earth.

While a desert can present a uniquely challenging environment, the scarcity of roads means navigation couldn't be simpler. For the first ride you head out of the town of Mitzpe Ramon, down the hairpins and south on Highway 40 for 85km (53 miles) to Neot Smadar, where the excellent roadside *pundak* (Hebrew for 'inn') of the same name awaits.

Mitzpe Ramon sits on the Ramon Crater, which wasn't actually formed by a volcano or meteor strike but, unusually, by erosion. This whole area was once covered by an ocean, but 220 million years, it would seem, can do this to a place.

As you head out of town, it's so quiet it's almost eerie. The 40km- (25 mile-) long Ramon Crater is desolate, as unchanging as a photograph. For a moment it feels like the world has been frozen, but as you point your bike downhill and begin to pick up speed, life restarts in a rush of sound and colour. The dotted white line in the middle of the road becomes a blur, and the switchbacks wouldn't look out of place on a racetrack. By the time you reach the crater floor, 350m (1,148ft) below, you've already notched up 10km (6 miles) in a matter of minutes. It's one exceptionally fast road, thanks to a net vertical loss of 568m (1,863ft), which is something you can reflect on as you tuck into stuffed vine leaves and dips too innumerable to list at the Pundak Neot Smadar.

The second ride involves heading for the Dead Sea in your support vehicle and starting from the resort of Ein Bokek. You follow Highway 90 south along the shore, and soon the hotels >>

Ein Bokek

Scorpions Pass

Route 227

Mitzpe Ramon

Highway 40

Neot Smadar

RIDE 1
Distance: 86km *(53 miles)*
Elevation loss: 1,038m *(3,405ft)*

RIDE 2
Distance: 173km *(107 miles)*
Elevation gain: 1,902m *(6,240ft)*

Soon the hotels give way to unspoiled views across the water to Jordan

>> give way to unspoiled views across the water to Jordan. The sea is still, but appears to be thick as syrup.

Your bike computer will soon register –394m (–1,293ft) and, given that the road looks to be climbing and swinging inland, it would appear you've found yourself on the lowest paved road on Earth. You're here because the Dead Sea is receding dramatically. When it was measured in the 1950s, the sea was 80km (50 miles) long; today it's just 48km (30 miles).

Just after 50km (31 miles), take a right at the junction with signs for Be'er Sheva and Idan onto Route 227 towards Yeruham. Follow the road for 35km (22 miles) and up and over Ma'ale Akrabim, known in English as 'Scorpions Pass'. Despite its name, the dimensions of this 34-km (21-mile) pass, built by the Romans, don't initially sound fierce. The introductory section is a shallow 1% drag, and even when things get steeper the average incline doesn't nudge above 5%. But things do get hairier when a sign entitled 'Aqrabbim Ascent' points you right at a fork in the road. The asphalt is rutted and cracked from decades of searing sun, and the only thing separating you from vertigo-inducing drops is a series of rusted, sand-filled barrels spaced roughly every few metres (yards). It's a relief to be climbing and not descending as you wrest the bars through the hairpins to the summit, where the vast yellow desert reaches into the distance in all directions.

The road spikes again before it begins a meandering plunge back towards the Dead Sea, but even so you don't exceed 600m (1,968ft). The road merges into Route 206 and after 2km (1¼ miles) you turn right at the T-junction on Route 225 to Yeruham – a good place to stop for a coffee – before taking Route 204 north towards Dimona. When you reach Route 25, you head east for 20km (12½ miles), then north on Route 258 towards the Nahal Abuv Nature Reserve. From there you descend Route 31 southeast back to Ein Bokek and a float in the Dead Sea.

Along the way, coarse scrub springs defiantly from the sandy floor. Anywhere else these plants would be a dull mottle of greens, but for eyes attuned to the yellow of the desert they're a luminous feast in the fading light, and a fitting end to a magnificent ride.

UNITED STATES
Hawaii

Mauna Kea on the island of Hawaii lays claim to being the hardest climb
on Earth. At the very least it will give you a brutal day in the saddle.

Distance: 92km *(57 miles)*
Elevation: 4,192m *(13,753ft)*

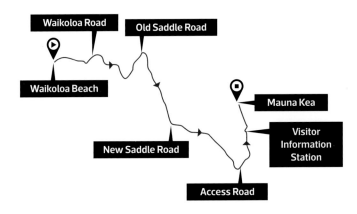

On most mornings, for just a few minutes after sunrise, from the western shores of Hawaii you can make out the top of Mauna Kea, the grand volcanic peak hanging over the island like some prehistoric monster. Then it's gone – concealed by a mist that turns the sky into an orange haze.

Mauna Kea, technically the tallest mountain on Earth, stands over 10,000m (32,808ft) high when measured from its true base in the ocean. From the water's edge on Waikoloa Beach, the summit is 4,192m (13,753ft) above you, and the road to it is considered to be the hardest cycling climb on the planet. The journey is 92km (57 miles) long, during which there is just a single 1-km (2/3-mile) downhill segment. The rest is climbing, with a 24-km (15-mile) stretch at 9%, a 12-km (7½-mile) stretch at 12% and a rolling 16-km (10-mile) stretch at 7% with back-to-back spikes of 15%. That's before you get near the summit, where you can expect long chunks at 20%. Some of it on gravel. All of it at high altitude.

The ride starts from Waikoloa Beach. You ride on State Route 19, the main coastal highway, and by the time you reach the town of Waikoloa you've already travelled 13km (8 miles) uphill and watched the landscape switch from tropical beaches to open plains of grass and rock.

After another 22km (14 miles) you turn left onto the Mamalahoa Highway, which offers a few kilometres' relief from the wind that whips the coast, and then turn right onto the Old Saddle Road. The next 16km (10 miles) is at a 6% average, which would be the main climb of the day if you were in the Alps. To your right the Pacific Ocean is now 1.6km (1 mile) below you.

Eventually you turn onto the New Saddle Road. This section of the climb is 22km (14 miles) at 4%, which is by no means steep. However, the worsening wind will chip away at your energy reserves. The landscape changes again, this time into a barren plain of black lava, the lingering remnants of the Mauna Ulu lava flow in 1969.

You're 70km (43½ miles) into the ride, and from here the road snakes up with violent steepness towards the Visitor Information Station. This first part of the Access Road, or John A. Burns Way, is 10km (6 miles) at 9% with lengthy spikes of 15%. Beyond that is the crowning glory of the whole climb, in the form of a restricted part-gravel road to the observatory atop Mauna Kea. In all, it means you still face an ascent of 2,200m (7,218ft) over 24km (15 miles).   >>

>> You soon see a ramp of 10% and, worse, you quickly realize that the incline is here to stay. You'll track from one verge to the other as you attempt to find a manageable gradient. But make no mistake. The road is stubborn, and it refuses to relent from its upward progress even for a second.

The Visitor Centre at 2,800m (9,186ft) is higher than any Alpine pass, but Mauna Kea isn't finished with you yet because this is where the second part of the John A. Burns Way begins. The next 7km (4⅓ miles) averages above 11% and is littered with lengthy 20% gravel ramps. Beyond that the gradient intensifies even more. Only 4x4 vehicles are allowed up here, so keeping traction on just two wheels powered by protesting muscles isn't easy. You may find yourself having to walk at times, so dry and fine is the road surface.

All around you, life seems to have given up. Where before there were shrubs and flowers, the air is now too thin for animal and plant life to survive. It's a moonscape, but the end of the gravel isn't the end of the climb. You're just above 3,500m (11,482ft), yet ahead of you is still 7km (4⅓ miles) of climbing, much of it at well over 10% – a monster in its own right. At this altitude the landscape is all the more surreal. The ground is like a coral red desert of stones, while on the horizon are volcanic craters that glint with the sun's blinding reflection. It's as if you're on a different planet.

The final few hundred metres up to the observatory are pure torture, and this is definitely not a ride for the faint-hearted. You will probably be climbing for at least 10 hours and you may need someone to bring you back down the mountain by 4x4 if you display symptoms of altitude sickness.

But the view from the top of Mauna Kea has no equal. Immense vistas of ocean are spread out across the horizon. In the foreground, the vast peak of Mauna Loa sits just below a low sun, beside which the volcanic billows of the Kilauea lava flow diffuse into the sky. The Polynesians who first set foot on Mauna Kea considered it the summit of the universe and, sitting here on a bike, it's impossible to disagree.

It's like you're on a different planet

Index

Writing credits (page numbers refer to the first page of the ride):

20, 24, 78, 94, 102, 218 Mark Bailey; 90 Matt Barbet; 56, 82, 146, 174, 184 Stu Bowers; 12, 16, 32, 44, 74, 98 Henry Catchpole; 126 Michael Cotty; 114 Joshua Cunningham; 68 Wesley Doyle; 142, 200 Pete Muir; 40, 178 Susannah Osborne; 154 Steve Prentice; 28, 60, 118, 150, 166, 192, 212 James Spender; 48, 86, 130, 138, 162, 170, 188, 196, 204, 208 Peter Stuart; 36, 64, 106, 110 Trevor Ward; 52, 134, 158 Steve Westlake.

Photography credits (page numbers refer to the first page of the ride):

12, 16, 24, 32, 36, 44, 74, 78, 90, 94, 106, 126, 184 Paul Calver; 40, 52, 64, 134 Richie Hopson; 82, 200 Patrik Lundin; 114, 118 George Marshall; 212 Mike Massaro; 192, 196, 208 Rob Milton; 28, 48, 56, 60, 86, 98, 102, 110, 130, 138, 142, 150, 158, 162, 166, 178, 218 Juan Trujillo Andrades; 68, 154, 170, 188, 204 Geoff Waugh; 20 Pete Webb; 146, 174 Wig Worland.

An Hachette UK Company
www.hachette.co.uk

First published in Great Britain in 2020 by Mitchell Beazley,
an imprint of Octopus Publishing Group Ltd, Carmelite House,
50 Victoria Embankment, London EC4Y 0DZ
www.octopusbooks.co.uk

Distributed in the US by Hachette Book Group,
1290 Avenue of the Americas, 4th and 5th Floors, New York, NY 10104

Distributed in Canada by Canadian Manda Group, 664 Annette St,
Toronto, Ontario, Canada M6S 2C8

ISBN 978-1-78472-687-4

A CIP catalogue record for this book is available from the British Library.

Printed and bound in China.

10 8 6 4 2 1 3 5 7 9

Disclaimer: All routes were open at the time of going to press,
but please check for road closures before setting out on a ride.

Text compiled by: Michael Donlevy
Commissioning Editor: Joe Cottington
Art Director: Juliette Norsworthy
Designer: Chapel
Senior Editor: Leanne Bryan
Production Controller: Emily Noto

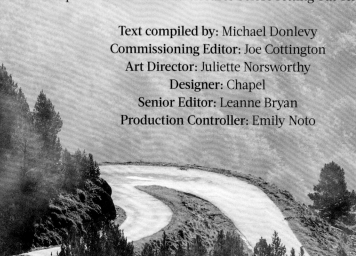